Easy Learning

Design Patterns

Java

(3 Edition)

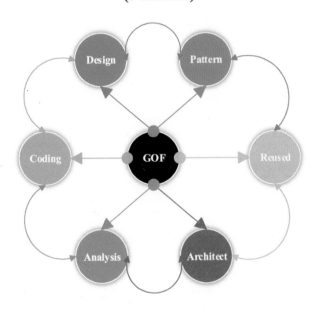

YANG HU

Build Clean and Reusable Object-Oriented Code.

http://en.verejava.com

ISBN: 9798726938677

CONTENTS

If you want to learn this book, you must have basic knowledge of Java, you can learn book: << Easy Learning Java(4 Edition)>>
https://www.amazon.com/dp/B08ZDB8NDH

If you already have basic knowledge of Java, skip it, start an exciting journey

Download DesginPatternsImage.zip all images for this book.
http://en.verejava.com/download.jsp?id=1

Introduction to Design Patterns

Design Patterns: are reusable solutions to commonly occuring problems. Design patterns were started as best practices that were applied again and again to similar problems encountered in different contexts. It is a description or template for how to solve a problem that can be used in many different situations.

The purpose of learning design patterns: let you write beautiful and clean code. Reasonable use of design patterns can improve software development reusability, and improve code reuse and scalability.

There are 3 categories of design patterns: Creational Patterns, Structural Patterns, Behavioural Patterns

    1. Creational Patterns: provide ways to instantiate single objects or groups of related objects.

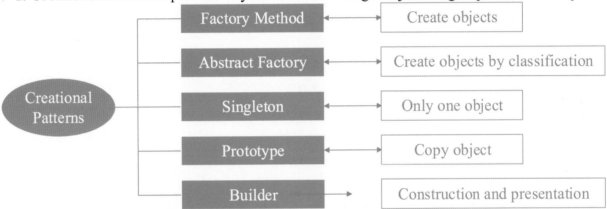

2. Structural Patterns: provide a manner to define relationships between classes or objects.

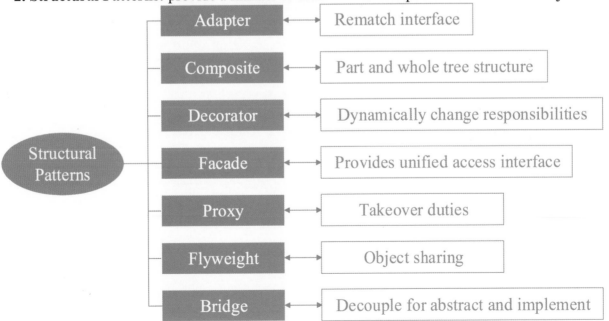

3. Behavioural Patterns: define manners of communication between classes and objects.

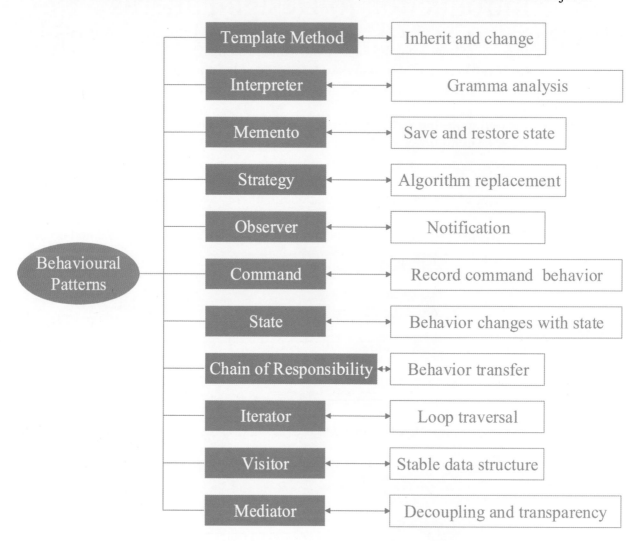

Introduction to Class Diagram in UML

UML: Unified Modeling Language, is a standardized modeling language consisting of an integrated set of diagrams, developed to help system and software developers for specifying, visualizing, constructing, and documenting the artifacts of software systems. The UML is a very important part of developing object oriented software and the software development process. The UML uses mostly graphical notations to express the design of software projects.

This book is divided into 2 parts:
   1. Design Pattern Principle: Explain the principle of design pattern in an easy-to-understand way.
   2. Design Pattern Practice: Interpret design patterns based on practice.

In this chapter, we will give you details about what is the basic concepts of UML class diagram to help you continue the next step of learning.

Class Diagram:
A class diagram models the static structure of a system. It shows relationships between classes, objects, attributes, and operations.

1. Composition: The relationship strong can not separate between 2 classes
2. Aggregation: The relationship weak can not separate between 2 classes
3. Association: Ownership between 2 classes
4. Dependence: Use relationship between 2 classes
5. Generalization: Inheritance relationship between 2 classes
6. Implementation: Interface and implementation relationship

1. Composition Example: Mother is pregnant contains a fetus

Mother and Fetus the relationship strong can not separate, if the mother dies, the fetus will die.

Generally composition relationship use member variable and inner class to represent.

Solid diamonds are used to represent Composition relationships

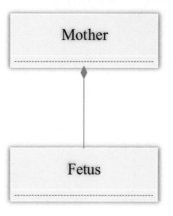

```
class Mother {
   private Fetus fetus;

   public Mother(){
      this.fetus = new Fetus();
   }

   class Fetus{

   }
}
```

2. Aggregation Example: Mother has a newborn baby

Mother and NewBorn the relationship weak can not separate. The newborn needs mother all the time, but if the mother dies, the newborn may not die.

Generally aggregation relationship use member variable to represent.

Hollow diamonds are used to represent Aggregation relationships

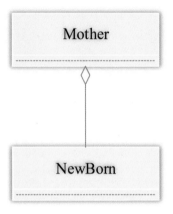

```
class NewBorn{

}

class Mother {
    private NewBorn newBorn;

    public Mother(NewBorn newBorn){
        this.newBorn = newBorn;
    }
}
```

3. Association Example: Mother has a 4 year old todder

Mother has a 4-year-old Todder, the relationship between Mother and Todder is not as strong as before, and the Todder can play and walk by himself.

Generally association relationship use member variable to represent.

A solid line with an arrow indicates an association relationship

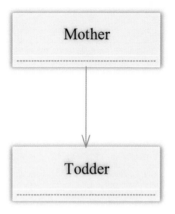

```
class Todder{

}

class Mother {
    private Todder todder;

    public void setTodder(Todder todder){
        this.todder = todder;
    }
}
```

4. Dependence Example: Mother sometimes need her 8 years old child help sweep, in fact mother can also do it herself.

Dependency relationship means that Mother class depends on the definition of child class. Generally, the dependency relationship is reflected as a local variable.
Dotted lines with arrows indicate dependencies

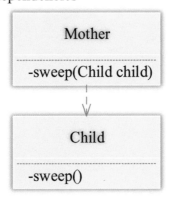

Create a test file: TestDependency.java

```java
class Child{
    public void sweep(){
        System.out.println("I can help sweep");
    }
}

class Mother {
    //Mother depends on the definition of Child as a local variable.
    public void sweep(Child child){
        child.sweep();
    }
}

public class TestDependency {
    public static void main(String[] args) {
        Mother mother = new Mother();
        mother.sweep(new Child());
    }
}
```

Result:
I can help sweep

From the above example, As the child grows up, the dependence between the child and the mother gradually weakens.
The strength of relationship: Composition > Aggregation > Association > Dependence

5. Generalization Example: Human can speak, man also can speak

Human can speak, Man also can speak, this means Man inherit from Human the ability.

The solid line with a triangular arrow indicates the inheritance relationship

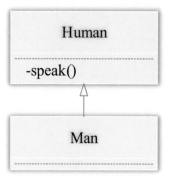

Create a test file: TestGeneralization.java

```java
class Human{

    public void speak(){
        System.out.println("Human can speak");
    }
}

class Man extends Human{

}

public class TestGeneralization {
    public static void main(String[] args) {
        Man man = new Man();
        man.speak();
    }
}
```

Result:
Human can speak

6. Implementation Example: Mother told her son to buy fruit.

Mother wanted to buy fruit, didn't do it, but let the Son do it.

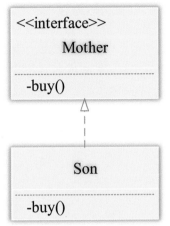

Create a test file: TestImplementation.java

```java
interface Mother{

    public void buy(); //Mother wanted to buy fruit, didn't do it
}

class Son implements Mother{

    //let the Son do it
    public void buy(){
        System.out.println("I will help buy fruit");
    }
}

public class TestImplementation {
    public static void main(String[] args) {
        Mother mother = new Son();
        mother.buy();
    }
}
```

Result:
I will help buy fruit

Open Closed Principle

Open closed principle: states that a module should be open to extension but closed for modification.

Open for extension: This means that the behavior of the module can be extended. As the requirements of the application change, we are able to extend the module with new behaviors that satisfy those changes.

Closed for modification: Extending the behavior of a module does not result in changes to the source code.

1. Example: mathematical operation program with Open closed principle

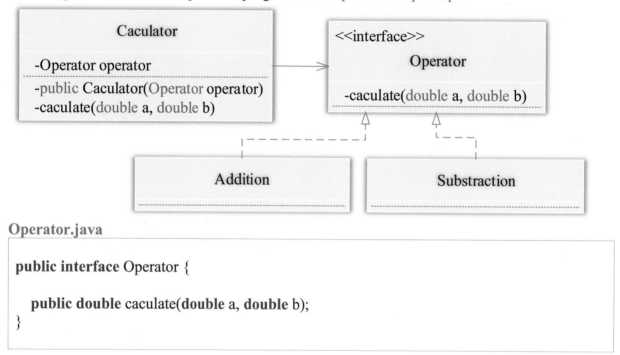

Operator.java

```java
public interface Operator {

    public double caculate(double a, double b);
}
```

Addition.java

```java
public class Addition implements Operator{

    public double caculate(double a, double b){
        return a + b;
    }
}
```

Substraction.java

```java
public class Substraction implements Operator{

   public double caculate(double a, double b){
      return a - b;
   }
}
```

Caculator.java

```java
public class Caculator {
   private Operator operator;

   public Caculator(Operator operator){
      this.operator = operator;
   }

   public double caculate(double a, double b){

      return operator.caculate(a, b);
   }
}
```

If we need to add a Multiplication class, we don't need to modify the Caculator class. So this design meet the Open Closed Principle and benefit for extension.

The subsequent chapters will gradually apply design patterns to GUI Swing game development. We need to use some knowledge of GUI Swing, animation and game development. In the following sections, let's lean this knowledge in advance.

Create GUI Window Application

Java offers Swing for developing GUI (Graphical User Interface). Swing is the most commonly used. It is a standard Java interface to the GUI toolkit. Java with Swing is the fastest and easiest way to create the GUI applications.

1.Create a file : AirplaneGame.java in Eclipse

JFrame: class is a type of container can create a window.
JFrame.setSize(int width, int height): set the size of the frame.
JFrame.setVisible(true): set visible of the frame to open a window.
import javax.swing.* : provides classes for java swing GUI API.

```java
import javax.swing.*;
public class AirplaneGame {
    public static void main(String[] args) {
        JFrame frame = new JFrame("Java GUI Application");
        frame.setSize(300,300);
        frame.setVisible(true);
    }
}
```

Run as -> Java Application Open a window:

Create Canvas

Canvas: is used to draw graphics and image on screen. The Java library includes a simple package for drawing 2D graphics, called java.awt

There are several ways to create graphics in Java; we can create Canvas inherit from JPanel, A Canvas is a blank rectangular area of the screen onto which the application can draw.

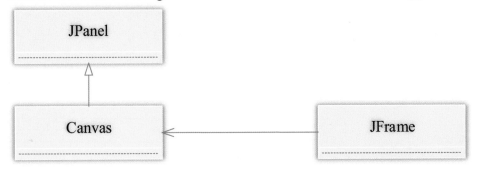

1. Create a Canvas inherit from JPanel and then add this canvas to the center of JFrame.

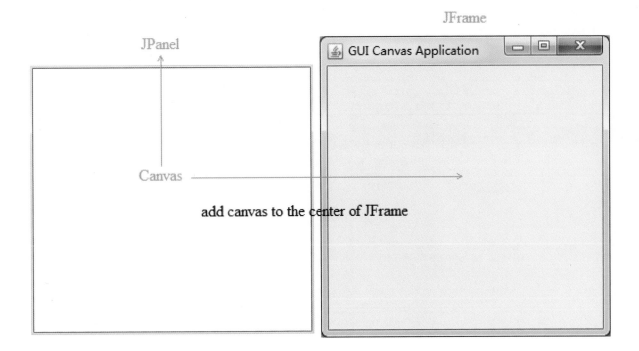

1. Create a file : AirplaneGame.java in Eclipse
this.setLayout(null): must set layout null
this.setBackground(Color c): set the background color in a JPanel

```java
import javax.swing.*;
import java.awt.*;

class Canvas extends JPanel{
   public Canvas(){
      this.setLayout(null);
      this.setBackground(Color.WHITE); // set the background color: white
   }
}

public class AirplaneGame {
   public static void main(String[] args) {
      JFrame frame = new JFrame("GUI Canvas Application");
      Canvas canvas = new Canvas();
      frame.add(canvas);  // add canvas to the center of JFrame
      frame.setSize(300,300);
      frame.setVisible(true);
   }
}
```

Run as -> Java Application Open a window:

16

Graphics Draw on Canvas

The Graphics class provides basic drawing methods such as: drawLine, drawRect, drawString and drawImage.

When we want to draw our own graphics on the screen, we should put our graphics code inside the paintComponent() method in JPanel. The system calls it directly. So our Canvas need to override this paintComponent() method to perform our graphics code.

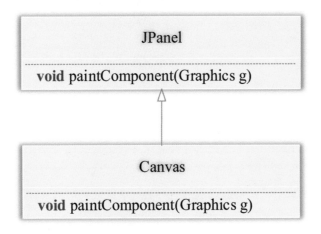

```
class Canvas extends JPanel{

    public Canvas(){
        this.setLayout(null);
        this.setBackground(Color.WHITE);
    }

    protected void paintComponent(Graphics g){
        super.paintComponent(g);
        // put our graphics code here
    }
}
```

1. Draw a line on Canvas

Java uses a coordinate system where the origin is in the upper-left corner. Graphical coordinates are measured in pixels; each pixel corresponds to a dot on the screen.

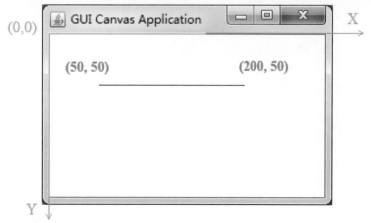

g.drawLine(x1, y1, x2, y2): takes four integers values that represent the start (x1, y1) and end (x2, y2) coordinate of the line.

```java
import javax.swing.*;
import java.awt.*;

class Canvas extends JPanel{
    public Canvas(){
        this.setLayout(null);
        this.setBackground(Color.WHITE); // set the background color: white
    }

    protected void paintComponent(Graphics g){
        super.paintComponent(g);
        g.drawLine(50, 50, 200, 50); // draw a line from (50,50) to (200,50)
    }
}

public class AirplaneGame {
    public static void main(String[] args) {
        JFrame frame = new JFrame("GUI Canvas Application");
        Canvas canvas = new Canvas();
        frame.add(canvas);  // add canvas to the center of JFrame
        frame.setSize(300,200);
        frame.setVisible(true);
    }
}
```

2. Draw a Rectangle on Canvas

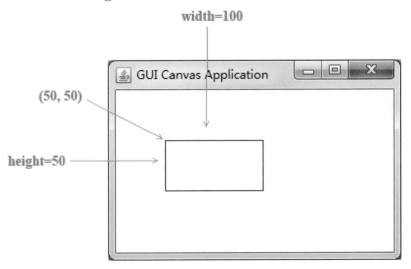

g. drawRect(int x, int y, int width, int height): draw a rectangle on the canvas.

```java
import java.awt.*;
import javax.swing.*;
class Canvas extends JPanel{

    public Canvas(){
        this.setLayout(null);
        this.setBackground(Color.WHITE);
    }

    protected void paintComponent(Graphics g){
        super.paintComponent(g);
        g.drawRect(50, 50, 100, 50); // draw a Rect from (50,50),width=100 height=50
    }
}

public class AirplaneGame {
    public static void main(String[] args) {
        JFrame frame = new JFrame("GUI Canvas Application");
        Canvas canvas = new Canvas();
        frame.add(canvas);
        frame.setSize(300,200);
        frame.setVisible(true);
    }
}
```

3. Fill a Rectangle on Canvas

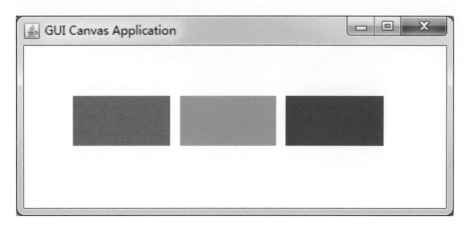

g. fillRect(int x, int y, int width, int height): fill a rectangle on the canvas.
g.setColor(Color c): the color (red: Color.RED, green: Color.GREEN, blue: Color.BLUE).

```java
import java.awt.*;
import javax.swing.*;

class Canvas extends JPanel{
    public Canvas(){
        this.setLayout(null);
        this.setBackground(Color.WHITE);
    }

    protected void paintComponent(Graphics g){
        super.paintComponent(g);
        // draw a red Rect
        g.setColor(Color.RED);
        g.fillRect(50, 50, 100, 50);

        // draw a green Rect
        g.setColor(Color.GREEN);
        g.fillRect(160, 50, 100, 50);

        // draw a blue Rect
        g.setColor(Color.BLUE);
        g.fillRect(270, 50, 100, 50);
    }
}
```

4. Draw a image on canvas.

All images in DesignPatternsImages.zip please find download from this link:

http://en.verejava.com/download.jsp?id=1

put the images to Project test/images

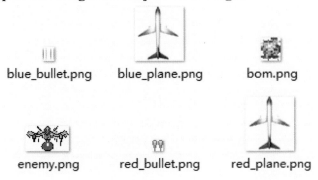

blue_bullet.png   blue_plane.png   bom.png

enemy.png   red_bullet.png   red_plane.png

Project test/images

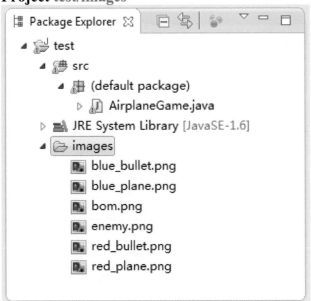

draw images/blue_plane.png **on canvas.**

1. Create a method to load image from test/images/blue_plane.png to BufferedImage

new File(imagePath): create a file object by image path.
ImageIO.read(file): read a image file save to BufferedImage
g.drawImage(image, x, y, null): draw a image to canvas

2. Draw BufferedImage on canvas

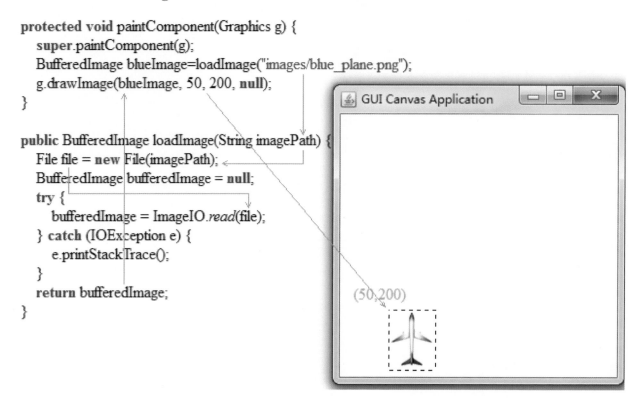

```
protected void paintComponent(Graphics g) {
    super.paintComponent(g);
    BufferedImage blueImage=loadImage("images/blue_plane.png");
    g.drawImage(blueImage, 50, 200, null);
}

public BufferedImage loadImage(String imagePath) {
    File file = new File(imagePath);
    BufferedImage bufferedImage = null;
    try {
        bufferedImage = ImageIO.read(file);
    } catch (IOException e) {
        e.printStackTrace();
    }
    return bufferedImage;
}
```

22

Create a file: AirplaneGame.java **in Eclipse**

```java
import java.awt.*;
import java.awt.image.BufferedImage;
import java.io.*;
import javax.imageio.ImageIO;
import javax.swing.*;

class Canvas extends JPanel{
  public Canvas(){
    this.setLayout(null);
    this.setBackground(Color.WHITE); // set the background color: white
  }

  protected void paintComponent(Graphics g) {
    super.paintComponent(g);
    BufferedImage blueImage=loadImage("images/blue_plane.png");
    g.drawImage(blueImage, 50, 200, null);
  }

  public BufferedImage loadImage(String imagePath) {
    File file = new File(imagePath);
    BufferedImage bufferedImage = null;
    try {
      bufferedImage = ImageIO.read(file);
    } catch (IOException e) {
      e.printStackTrace();
    }
    return bufferedImage;
  }
}

public class AirplaneGame {
  public static void main(String[] args) {
    JFrame frame = new JFrame("GUI Canvas Application");
    Canvas canvas = new Canvas();
    frame.add(canvas);  // add canvas to the center of JFrame
    frame.setSize(300,300);
    frame.setVisible(true);
  }
}
```

Animation

1. The enemy plane load image draw on the top of Canvas, and then moves down automatically.

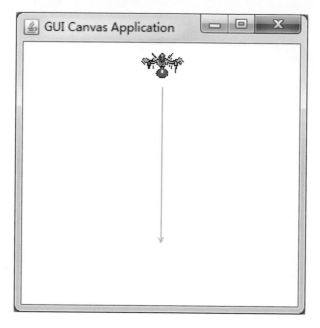

Analysis:

   1. Class: EnemyPlane, Canvas

   2. Relationship:

      2.1 Enemy plane draw on the top of Canvas: This means EnemyPlane belong to Canvas

  3. Attributes:

   3.1 Enemy plane load image: this mean EnemyPlane has image and the width and height of image attribute.

   3.2 Enemy plane draw on Canvas: this mean EnemyPlane has x,y coordinates.

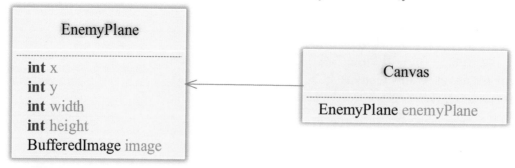

4. Methods:

4.1 Enemy plane need load image: we can create a class ImageUtil and a method BufferedImage loadImage(String imagePath) to load image, we can create a constructor method EnemyPlane(int x, int y, String imagePath) pass the imagePath and then call the loadImage(String imagePath) to load image.

```java
public EnemyPlane(int x, int y, String imagePath){
    this.x = x;
    this.y = y;
    this.image=ImageUtil.loadImage(imagePath); // load image to BufferedImage
    this.width = this.image.getWidth();
    this.height = this.image.getHeight();
}
```

4.2 Enemy plane draw on the top of Canvas: we can create a method draw(Graphics g).

```java
public void draw(Graphics g){
    g.drawImage(image, this.x, this.y, null); // draw image on Canvas
}
```

4.3 Enemy plane moves down: we can create a method move(int distanceX, int distanceY) distanceX, int distanceY indicates the distance moved in the X and Y axis .

```java
public void move(int distanceX, int distanceY){
    this.x = this.x + distanceX;
    this.y = this.y + distanceY;
}
```

4.4 The attribute x, y, width, height has its own public getter and setter methods.

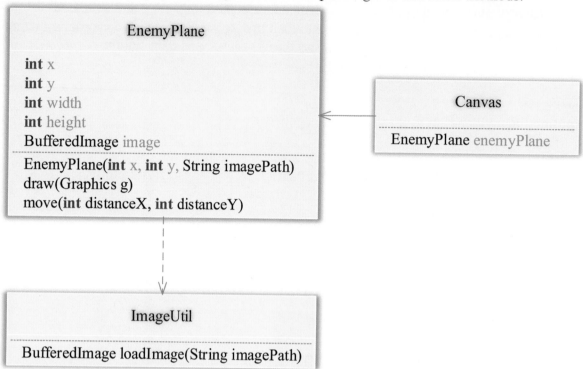

4.5 Enemy plane want to draw on the top of Canvas: we need create a constructor method Canvas() to initialize the enemy plane and then draw on the Canvas in method paintComponent(Graphics g) .

```java
public Canvas() {
    enemyPlane= new EnemyPlane(100, 0, "images/enemy.png");
}
```

```java
protected void paintComponent(Graphics g) {
    super.paintComponent(g);
    enemyPlane.draw(g);
    enemyPlane.move(0, 3); // enemy plane moves down 3 pixels
}
```

4.6 Enemy plane moves down automatically: We need define a inner class CanvasThread inherit from Thead in Canvas, there is a run() method. we can define "while (true)" where we repeatedly call draw(Graphics g) and move(int distanceX, int distanceY) to change the position of the enemy plane and then we call repaint(), which forces to call the paintComponent(Graphics g) method to paint again the canvas.

```java
protected void paintComponent(Graphics g){
    super.paintComponent(g);
    enemyPlane.draw(g);
    enemyPlane.move(0, 3);
}

class CanvasThread extends Thread{
    @Override
    public void run() {
        while(isRun){
            try {
                Thread.sleep(200); // Sleep for 200 milliseconds repaint canvas
                Canvas.this.repaint();
            } catch (InterruptedException e) {
                e.printStackTrace();
            }
        }
    }
}
```

repaint flowchart

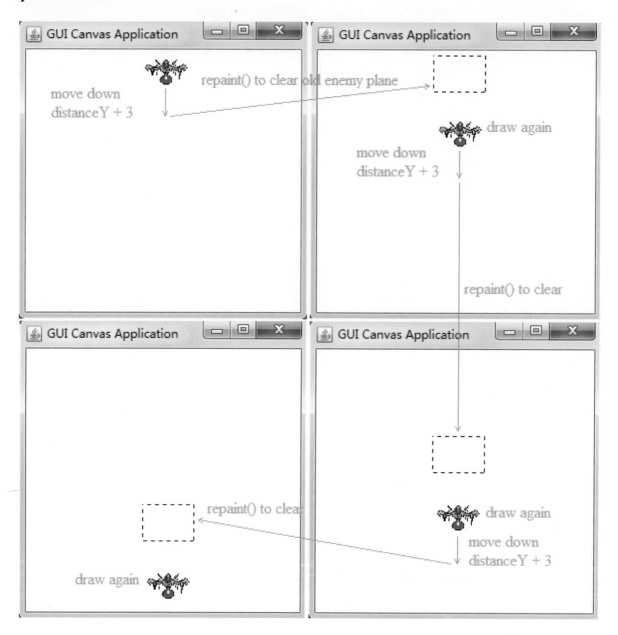

The final class diagram:

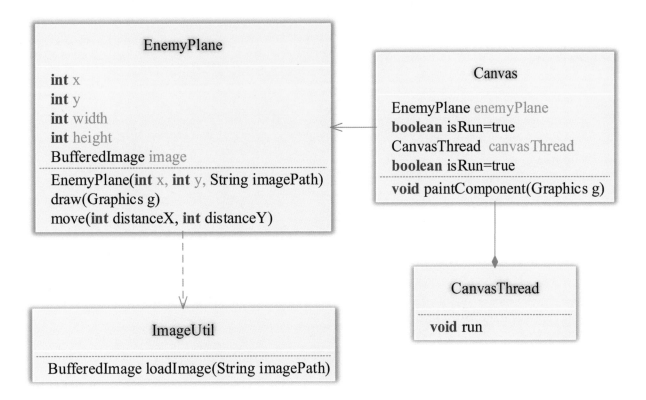

Create a Java Project: animation, and then create a class: ImageUtil to load image

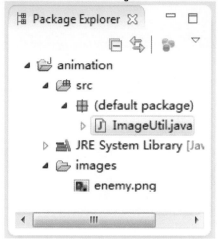

ImageUtil.java

```java
import java.awt.image.BufferedImage;
import java.io.*;
import javax.imageio.ImageIO;

public class ImageUtil {

    public static BufferedImage loadImage(String imagePath) {
        File file = new File(imagePath);
        BufferedImage bufferedImage = null;
        try {
            bufferedImage = ImageIO.read(file);
        } catch (IOException e) {
            e.printStackTrace();
        }
        return bufferedImage;
    }
}
```

Create a class: EnemyPlane.java

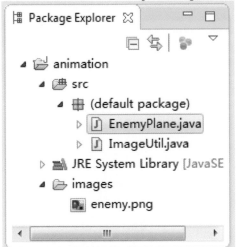

EnemyPlane.java

```java
import java.awt.Graphics;
import java.awt.image.BufferedImage;

public class EnemyPlane{
    protected int x;
    protected int y;
    protected BufferedImage image;
    protected int width;
    protected int height;

    public EnemyPlane(int x, int y, String imagePath){
        this.x = x;
        this.y = y;
        this.image=ImageUtil.loadImage(imagePath); // load image to BufferedImage
        this.width = this.image.getWidth();
        this.height = this.image.getHeight();
    }

    public void draw(Graphics g){
        g.drawImage(image, this.x, this.y, null); // draw image on Canvas
    }

    //Move a distance on the x,y axis
    public void move(int distanceX, int distanceY){
        this.x = this.x + distanceX;
        this.y = this.y + distanceY;
    }
```

```java
    public int getX() {
        return x;
    }

    public void setX(int x) {
        this.x = x;
    }

    public int getY() {
        return y;
    }

    public void setY(int y) {
        this.y = y;
    }

    public int getWidth() {
        return width;
    }

    public int getHeight() {
        return height;
    }
}
```

Create a class: Canvas.java to draw and move enemy plane

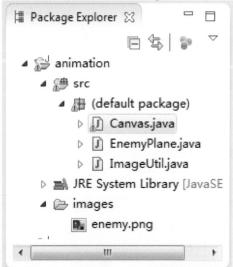

Canvas.java

```java
import java.awt.*;
import java.awt.event.*;
import java.awt.image.BufferedImage;
import java.io.*;
import java.util.*;
import javax.imageio.ImageIO;
import javax.swing.*;
public class Canvas extends JPanel {
    private EnemyPlane enemyPlane;
    private CanvasThread canvasThread; //inner class CanvasThread inherit from Thread
    private boolean isRun = true; // define "while (true)" where we repeatedly call  repaint()

    public Canvas() {
        this.setLayout(null);
        this.setBackground(Color.WHITE);
        this.requestFocus();
        enemyPlane= new EnemyPlane(100, 0, "images/enemy.png");
        canvasThread = new CanvasThread();
        canvasThread.start(); // start thread the run() method call automatically
    }

    protected void paintComponent(Graphics g) {
        super.paintComponent(g);
        enemyPlane.draw(g); // draw enemy plane
        enemyPlane.move(0, 3); // enemy plane moves down 3 pixels
    }

    class CanvasThread extends Thread{
        @Override
        public void run() {
            while(isRun){
                try {
                    Thread.sleep(200); // Sleep for 200 milliseconds repaint canvas
                    Canvas.this.repaint();
                } catch (InterruptedException e) {
                    e.printStackTrace();
                }
            }
        }
    }
}
```

Create a class: AirplaneGame.java to create a window and then add canvas to JFrame

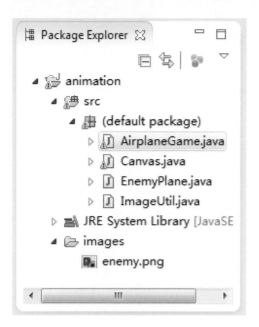

AirplaneGame.java

```java
import java.awt.*;
import javax.swing.*;

public class AirplaneGame {
    private static Canvas canvas;

    public static void main(String[] args) {
        JFrame frame = new JFrame("GUI Canvas Application");
        canvas = new Canvas();
        frame.add(canvas);
        frame.setSize(300, 300);
        frame.setVisible(true);
        canvas.requestFocus();
    }
}
```

Right click AirplaneGame.java, and then Run As –> Java Application

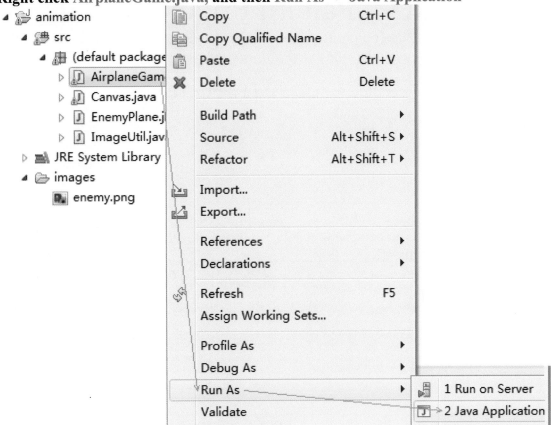

Result:

Strategy Pattern Principle

Strategy Pattern: Define a family of algorithms, encapsulates an algorithm inside a class., and make them interchangeable. Strategy lets the algorithm vary independently.

1. Example: E-commerce chooses different banks to pay different strategies

Analysis:

1. Create a interface: Strategy and then create a method: pay(double price)
2. Create 3 implementation class: MasterCard, VisaCard, Paypal
3. Create a class: PayManager to pass MasterCard, VisaCard, Paypal to pay different strategies

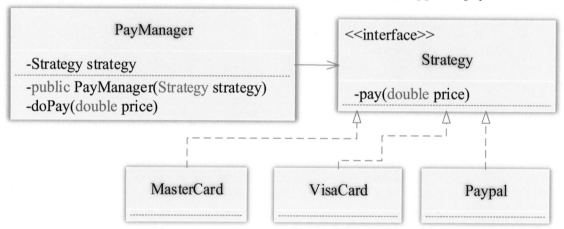

Create all classes in project test/com.strategy.principle

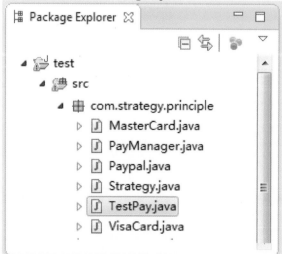

Strategy.java in package com.strategy.principle;

```java
public interface Strategy {

    public void pay(double price);
}
```

MasterCard.java in package com.strategy.principle;

```java
public class MasterCard implements Strategy{

    public void pay(double price) {
        System.out.println("Pay "+price+" $ by MasterCard");
    }
}
```

VisaCard.java in package com.strategy.principle;

```java
public class VisaCard implements Strategy{

    public void pay(double price) {
        System.out.println("Pay "+price+" $ by VisaCard");
    }
}
```

Paypal.java in package com.strategy.principle;

```java
public class Paypal implements Strategy{

    public void pay(double price) {
        System.out.println("Pay "+price+" $ by Paypal");
    }
}
```

PayManager.java in package com.strategy.principle;

```java
public class PayManager {
    private Strategy strategy;

    public PayManager(Strategy strategy) {
        this.strategy = strategy;
    }

    public void doPay(double price) {
        strategy.pay(price);
    }
}
```

2. Create a Test class : TestPay.java in package com.strategy.principle;

```java
import java.util.Scanner;
public class TestPay {
    public static void main(String[] args) {

        Scanner in = new Scanner(System.in);
        System.out.println("You need to pay $25  for mobile phone");
        System.out.println("Please select payment method 1: MasterCard 2: VisaCard 3:
Paypal");

        int code = in.nextInt();
        PayManager payManager = null;
        if (code == 1) {
            payManager = new PayManager(new MasterCard());
        } else if (code == 2) {
            payManager = new PayManager(new VisaCard());
        } else if (code == 3) {
            payManager = new PayManager(new Paypal());
        }

        payManager.doPay(25);
    }
}
```

Right click TestPay.java, and then Run As –> Java Application
Please input 1 Result:

```
Console ☒
<terminated> TestPay (2) [Java Application] C:\Program Files (x86)\Java\jre6\bin\javaw.exe (2021年2月
You need to pay $25   for mobile phone
Please select payment method 1: MasterCard 2: VisaCard 3: Paypal
1
Pay 25.0 $ by MasterCard
```

Run Again Please input 2 Result:

```
Console ☒
<terminated> TestPay (2) [Java Application] C:\Program Files (x86)\Java\jre6\bin\javaw.exe (2021年2月
You need to pay $25   for mobile phone
Please select payment method 1: MasterCard 2: VisaCard 3: Paypal
2
Pay 25.0 $ by VisaCard
```

Run Again Please input 3 Result:

```
Console ☒
<terminated> TestPay (2) [Java Application] C:\Program Files (x86)\Java\jre6\bin\javaw.exe (2021年2月
You need to pay $25   for mobile phone
Please select payment method 1: MasterCard 2: VisaCard 3: Paypal
3
Pay 25.0 $ by Paypal
```

Advantage of Strategy Pattern:
1. Meet the Open Closed Principle. If we need to add a ApplePay class, we don't need to modify the PayManager class.
2. Can improve the confidentiality and security of the strategy algorithm.

Disadvantages of Strategy Pattern:
1. The client must know all the strategies and decide which strategy class to use.

Strategy Pattern Case

Example: The enemy plane load image draw on the top of Canvas.
According to different strategies, enemy plane can move straight down,
enemy plane also can move slash down or move in other strategies of trajectories

Enemy plane move straight down

Enemy plane move slash down

Analysis:

1. Create a abstract class: MoveStrategy
and then declare an abstract method: move(**int** x, **int** y) to change the x, y coordinates of the enemy plane to change the trajectory.

```
public abstract void move(int x, int y);
```

2. Create an implementation class: MoveStraightDown for enemy plane move straight down

```
public void move(int x, int y) {
    this.resultX = x;
    this.resultY = y + 3; // Move down 3 pixels at a time
}
```

3. Create an implementation class: MoveSlashDown for enemy plane move slash down.

```
public void move(int x, int y) {
    this.resultX = x + 3; // Move right 3 pixels at a time
    this.resultY = y + 3; // Move down 3 pixels at a time
}
```

4. MoveStrategy as a member variable of EnemyPlane, EnemyPlane uses the method setMoveStrategy(MoveStrategy moveStrategy) to set its strategy of movement.

```
enemyPlane= new EnemyPlane(100, 0, "images/enemy.png");
enemyPlane.setMoveStrategy(new MoveStraightDown());
```

Or

```
enemyPlane= new EnemyPlane(100, 0, "images/enemy.png");
enemyPlane.setMoveStrategy(new MoveSlashDown());
```

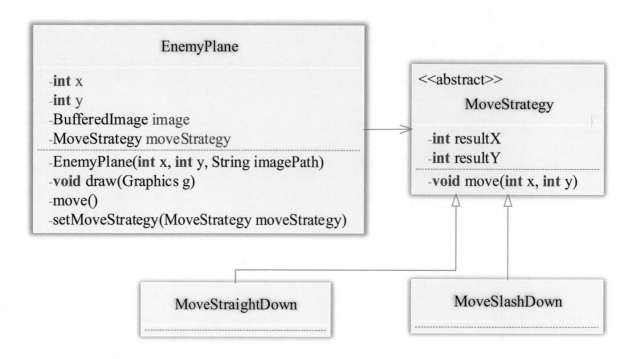

Meet the Open Closed Principle. If we add more Stragegy class, we don't need to modify the EnemyPlane class.

About Canvas, ImageUtil, CanvasThread repaint, please refer to the previous chapter **Animation**

Create all classes in project test/com.strategy.cases

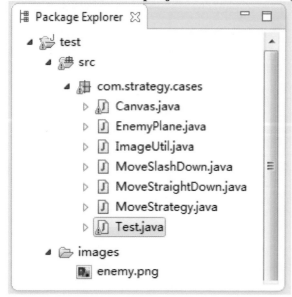

MoveStrategy.java in package com.strategy.cases;

```java
public abstract class MoveStrategy {
  protected int resultX;
  protected int resultY;

  public abstract void move(int x, int y);

  public int getResultX() {
    return resultX;
  }

  public int getResultY() {
    return resultY;
  }
}
```

MoveStraightDown.java in package com.strategy.cases;

```java
public class MoveStraightDown extends MoveStrategy{
  public void move(int x, int y) {
    this.resultX = x;
    this.resultY = y + 3; // Move down 3 pixels at a time
  }
}
```

MoveSlashDown.java in package com.strategy.cases;

```java
public class MoveSlashDown extends MoveStrategy{
  public void move(int x, int y) {
    this.resultX = x + 3; // Move right 3 pixels at a time
    this.resultY = y + 3; // Move down 3 pixels at a time
  }
}
```

Copy ImageUtil.java code here from the previous chapter: Animation

EnemyPlane.java in package com.strategy.cases;

```java
import java.awt.Graphics;
import java.awt.image.BufferedImage;

public class EnemyPlane{
    protected int x;
    protected int y;
    protected BufferedImage image;
    protected MoveStrategy moveStrategy;

    public EnemyPlane(int x, int y, String imagePath){
        this.x = x;
        this.y = y;
        this.image=ImageUtil.loadImage(imagePath); // load image to BufferedImage
    }

    public void draw(Graphics g){
        g.drawImage(image, this.x, this.y, null); // draw image on Canvas
    }

    public void move(){
        moveStrategy.move(this.x, this.y);
        // Assign the x, y result of the strategy to the x, y coordinates of the enemy plane
        this.x = moveStrategy.getResultX();
        this.y = moveStrategy.getResultY();
    }

    public void setMoveStrategy(MoveStrategy moveStrategy) {
        this.moveStrategy = moveStrategy;
    }
}
```

Canvas.java in package com.strategy.cases;

```java
import java.awt.*;
import java.awt.event.*;
import java.awt.image.BufferedImage;
import java.io.*;
import java.util.*;
import javax.imageio.ImageIO;
import javax.swing.*;
public class Canvas extends JPanel {
    private EnemyPlane enemyPlane;
    private CanvasThread canvasThread; //inner class CanvasThread inherit from Thread
    private boolean isRun = true; // define "while (true)" where we repeatedly call  repaint()

    public Canvas() {
        this.setLayout(null);
        this.setBackground(Color.WHITE);
        this.requestFocus();
        enemyPlane= new EnemyPlane(100, 0, "images/enemy.png");
        enemyPlane.setMoveStrategy(new MoveStraightDown());// set Stragety
        canvasThread = new CanvasThread();
        canvasThread.start(); // start thread the run() method call automatically
    }

    protected void paintComponent(Graphics g) {
        super.paintComponent(g);
        enemyPlane.draw(g); // draw enemy plane
        enemyPlane.move();
    }


    class CanvasThread extends Thread{
        public void run() {
            while(isRun){
                try {
                    Thread.sleep(200); // Sleep for 200 milliseconds repaint canvas
                    Canvas.this.repaint();
                } catch (InterruptedException e) {
                    e.printStackTrace();
                }
            }
        }
    }
}
```

Test.java in package com.strategy.cases;

```java
import java.awt.*;
import javax.swing.*;

public class Test {
    private static Canvas canvas;

    public static void main(String[] args) {
        JFrame frame = new JFrame("Test Strategy Pattern Case");
        canvas = new Canvas();
        frame.add(canvas);
        frame.setSize(300, 300);
        frame.setVisible(true);
        canvas.requestFocus();
    }
}
```

Right click Test.java, and then Run As –> Java Application in Eclipse

Enemy plane move straight down

Change MoveStrategy MoveStraightDown to MoveSlashDown in Canvas

```java
public Canvas() {

    enemyPlane= new EnemyPlane(100, 0, "images/enemy.png");
    enemyPlane.setMoveStrategy(new MoveSlashDown());

}
```

Right click Test.java, and then Run As –> Java Application in Eclipse

Enemy plane move slash down

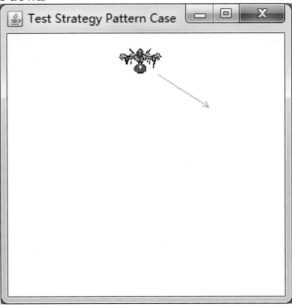

Composite Pattern Principle

Composite Pattern: A tree structure of simple and composite objects. Compose objects into tree structures to represent part-whole hierarchies.

1. Example: National city tree diagram

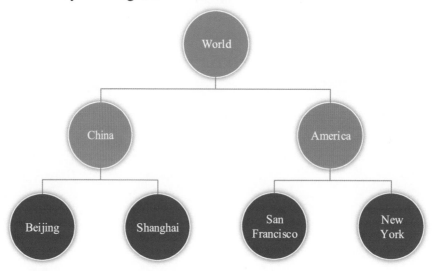

Analysis:

1. Each country and city are called node: Node
2. Each node has a attribute name: String name
3. The top node: **World** is called the root node of tree
4. There can be many child nodes under each node: List<Node> childNodes
    This means each node can add many child nodes: add(Node node)

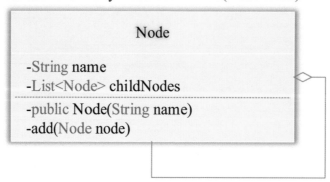

Advantage of Composite Pattern:

1. Can clearly define hierarchical complex objects, representing all or part of the object hierarchy, making it easier to add new components.

Create all classes in project test/com.composite.principle

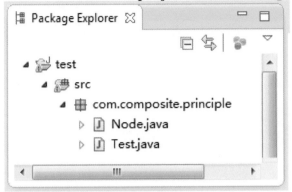

Node.java in package com.composite.principle;

```java
import java.util.*;

public class Node {

    protected String name;
    protected List<Node> childNodes;

    public Node(String name) {
        this.name = name;
        this.childNodes = new ArrayList<Node>();
    }

    // add child node to childNodes
    public void add(Node node) {
        childNodes.add(node);
    }

    public String getName() {
        return name;
    }

    public List<Node> getChildNodes() {
        return childNodes;
    }
}
```

3. Create a Test class : Test.java in package com.composite.principle;

```java
import java.util.List;
public class Test {
   public static void main(String[] args) {
      Node root=new Node("World"); // Create a root node

      Node china = new Node("China"); // Create a china node
      Node america = new Node("America"); // Create a america node
      root.add(china); // add china node to root
      root.add(america); // add america node to root

      Node beijing = new Node("Bei Jing");
      Node shanghai = new Node("Shang Hai");
      china.add(beijing);
      china.add(shanghai);

      Node sanfancisco = new Node("San Fancisco");
      Node newyork = new Node("New York");
      america.add(sanfancisco);
      america.add(newyork);

      // Print all nodes of the tree
      System.out.println(root.getName());
      List<Node> childeNodes = root.getChildNodes();
      for (Node node : childeNodes) {
         System.out.println("----" + node.getName());
         List<Node> childNodes2 = node.getChildNodes();
         for (Node node2 : childNodes2) {
            System.out.println("--------" + node2.getName());
         }
      }
   }
}
```

Right click Test.java, and then Run As –> Java Application Result:

```
Console ☒
World
----China
--------Bei Jing
--------Shang Hai
----America
--------San Fancisco
--------New York
```

Composite Pattern Case

Java File class is a Composite Pattern.

1. Example: Recursively print all directories and files in E:/books

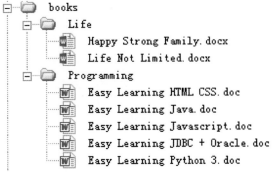

Analysis:

1. File and directory are called class File.
2. Each file and directory has a pathname.
3. There can be many child files and directories under directory.
4. There are some methods in File class.

File(String pathname)	Creates a new File instance by the pathname
File[] listFiles()	Returns an array of the file in the directory.
String getName()	Returns the name of the file or directory
boolean isDirectory()	Tests whether the file is a directory.
boolean isFile()	Tests whether the file is a normal file.
String getAbsolutePath()	Returns the absolute pathname

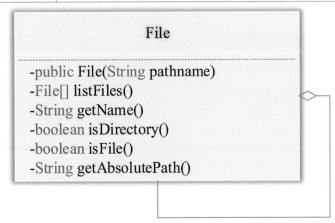

3. Create a Test class : TestFile.java in package com.composite.cases;

```java
import java.io.File;
public class TestFile {
    private static String level = "";

    public static void main(String[] args) {
        showAllDirectory("E:/books");
    }

    public static void showAllDirectory(String path) {
        File dir = new File(path);
        File[] dirs = dir.listFiles(); //List all child directories and files of the directory
        for (int i = 0; dirs != null && i < dirs.length; i++) {
            File f = dirs[i];
            if (f.isFile()) {
                System.out.println(level + f.getName());
            } else if (f.isDirectory()) {
                System.out.println(level + f.getName());
                level += "----";
                //Call recursively until all files and directories are printed
                showAllDirectory(f.getAbsolutePath());
                level = level.substring(0, level.lastIndexOf("----"));
            }
        }
    }
}
```

Right click TestFile.java, and then Run As –> Java Application Result:

```
Problems  @ Javadoc  Declaration  Console ⌧

Life
----Happy Strong Family.docx
----Life Not Limited.docx
Programming
----Easy Learning HTML CSS.doc
----Easy Learning Java.doc
----Easy Learning Javascript.doc
----Easy Learning JDBC + Oracle.doc
----Easy Learning Python 3.doc
```

Singleton Pattern Principle

Singleton Pattern: Ensure a class only has one instance, and provide a global point of access to it. The singleton has only one instance in the memory, which reduces memory costs

Analysis:
1. Create a class Singleton
2. To ensure Singleton has only one instance, set the member variable instance as static,

```
private static Singleton instance;
```

3. To prevent Singleton is instantiated externally through the constructor, set the constructor of the class to private.

```
private Singleton() {

}
```

4. Provide a global access method to get the same instance of the class

```
public static Singleton getInstance() {
   if (instance == null) {
      instance = new Singleton(); // there is only one instance
   }
   return instance;
}
```

Singleton
-**private static** Singleton *instance*
-**private** Singleton() -**public static** Singleton getInstance()

Singleton.java in package com.singleton.principle;

```java
public class Singleton {
    private static Singleton instance;

    private Singleton() {

    }

    public static Singleton getInstance() {
        if (instance == null) {
            instance = new Singleton(); // there is only one instance
        }
        return instance;
    }
}
```

2. Create a Test class : TestSingleton.java in package com.singleton.principle;

```java
public class TestSingleton {

    public static void main(String[] args) {
        Singleton s1 = Singleton.getInstance();
        Singleton s2 = Singleton.getInstance();

        // the two instances refer to the same address
        System.out.println(s1);
        System.out.println(s2);
    }
}
```

Right click TestSingleton.java, and then Run As –> Java Application Result:

```
Problems  @ Javadoc  Declaration  Console

<terminated> TestSingleton (1) [Java Application] C:\Program Files (x86)\Java\jre6\bin\javaw.exe (2019年
com.singleton.principle.Singleton@1f1fba0
com.singleton.principle.Singleton@1f1fba0
```

54

Singleton Pattern Case

Example:

When Java connects to the database, the parameters are often put into a configuration file: config.properties or xml. We can create a singleton class Config to read parameters from config.properties

UML Diagram

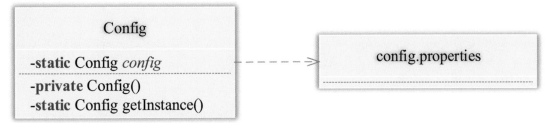

2. Create a file: config.properties in Eclipse project src

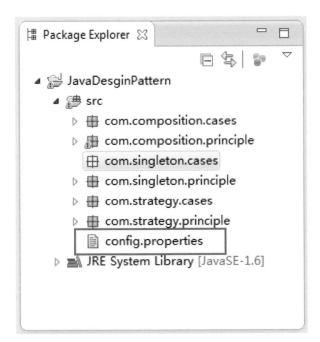

config.properties

Config.java in package com.singleton.cases;

```java
import java.io.*;
import java.util.Properties;

public class Config {
    private static Config config;
    private static Properties p = null;

    private Config() {
        try {
            if (p == null) {
                p = new Properties();
                InputStream is = this.getClass().getResourceAsStream("/config.properties");
                p.load(is); //Load config.properties
            }
        } catch (IOException e) {
            e.printStackTrace();
        }
    }

    public static Config getInstance() {
        if (config == null) {
            config = new Config(); //single instance
        }
        return config;
    }

    //Get the value by key
    public static String get(String key) {
        return p.getProperty(key);
    }
}
```

3. Create a Test class : TestConfig.java in package com.singleton.cases;

```java
public class TestConfig {

  public static void main(String[] args) {

    Config config1=Config.getInstance();
    System.out.println("Config1 Reference : "+config1);
    System.out.println(config1.get("classDriver"));
    System.out.println(config1.get("username"));
    System.out.println(config1.get("password"));

    System.out.println("--------------------------------------");

    Config config2=Config.getInstance();
    System.out.println("Config2 Reference : "+config2);
    System.out.println(config2.get("classDriver"));
    System.out.println(config2.get("username"));
    System.out.println(config2.get("password"));

  }
}
```

Right click TestConfig.java, and then Run As –> Java Application Result:

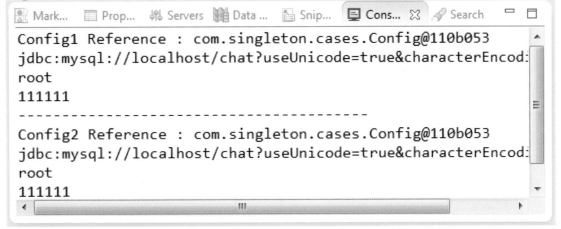

config1 and config2 got the same instance.

Template Method Pattern Principle

Template Method Pattern: Define the skeleton of an algorithm in a method, and delay some steps to subclasses. Template Method lets subclasses redefine some steps of an algorithm without changing the algorithm's structure.

1. Example: In the website, the head section, left section, and footer section are shared by each page, only the center section may be changed.
We can make the head section, left section, and footer section into a template, which is shared by each page, and only the center section will be changed for each page

LoginPage:

VereJava Copyright @ 2018 - 2020.

BookPage:

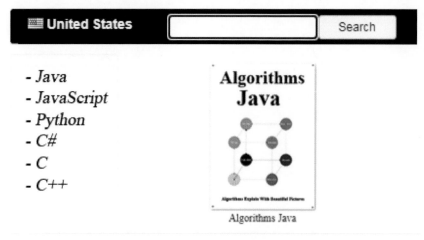

VereJava Copyright @ 2018 - 2020.

Analysis:

1. Create a Template class.
2. Create a public method show() to display head section, left section, and footer section.
3. Create a abstract method makeContent() for subclass: LoginPage, BookPage to extension.

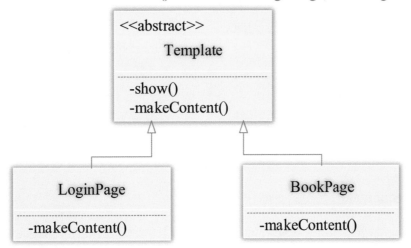

Template.java in package com.template.principle;

```java
public abstract class Template {

    public void show(){
        System.out.println("Content of head section");
        System.out.println("Content of left section");
        System.out.println("Content of footer section");

        makeContent();
    }

    public abstract void makeContent();
}
```

LoginPage.java in package com.template.principle;

```java
public class LoginPage extends Template {

    public void makeContent() {
        System.out.println("Content of login box");
    }
}
```

BookPage.java in package com.template.principle;

```java
public class BookPage extends Template {

    public void makeContent() {
        System.out.println("Content of Books");
    }
}
```

Create a Test class : Test.java in package com.template.principle;

```java
public class Test {

    public static void main(String[] args) {

        Template template = new LoginPage();
        template.show();

        System.out.println("------------------------");

        template = new BookPage();
        template.show();
    }
}
```

Right click Test.java, and then Run As –> Java Application Result:

```
Console ⊠
Content of head section
Content of left section
Content of footer section
Content of login box
--------------------------
Content of head section
Content of left section
Content of footer section
Content of Books
```

Template Pattern Case

Example:

Draw different rectangles on the canvas.

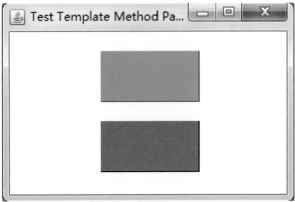

Analysis:

1. Create a abstract Template class: Rectangle.

2. Create a public method draw(Graphics g) to draw basic rectangle that shared by different rectangle.

3. Create a abstract method drawContent(Graphics g) for subclass: RedRectangle, GreenRectangle to extension.

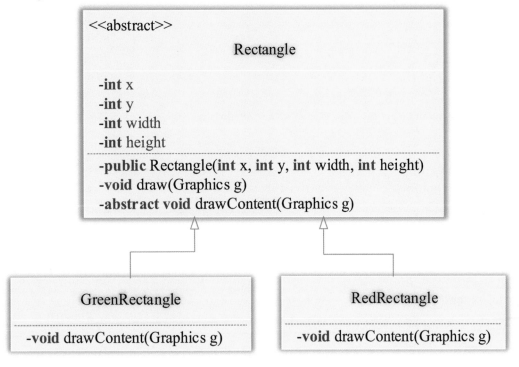

We can add more kinds of Rectangle to extend class: Rectange.

Create all classes in project test/com.template.cases

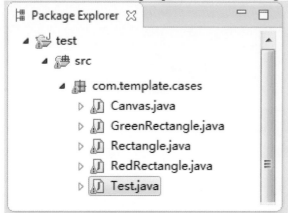

About Canvas, please refer to the previous chapter **Create Canvas**

Rectangle.java **in package** com.template.cases;

```java
import java.awt.Graphics;
import java.awt.image.BufferedImage;

public abstract class Rectangle{
    protected int x;
    protected int y;
    protected int width;
    protected int height;

    public Rectangle(int x, int y, int width, int height){
        this.x = x;
        this.y = y;
        this.width = width;
        this.height = height;
    }

    public void draw(Graphics g){
        g.drawRect(this.x, this.y, this.width, this.height);

        drawContent(g);
    }

    public abstract void drawContent(Graphics g);
}
```

GreenRectangle.java in package com.template.cases;

```java
import java.awt.*;
import java.awt.image.BufferedImage;

public  class GreenRectangle extends Rectangle{

    public GreenRectangle(int x, int y, int width, int height) {
        super(x, y, width, height);
    }

    public void drawContent(Graphics g){
        g.setColor(Color.GREEN); // set fill color to green
        g.fillRect(x, y, width, height);
        g.setColor(Color.BLACK); // restore the color to black
    }
}
```

RedRectangle.java in package com.template.cases;

```java
import java.awt.*;
import java.awt.image.BufferedImage;

public  class RedRectangle extends Rectangle{

    public RedRectangle(int x, int y, int width, int height) {
        super(x, y, width, height);
    }

    public void drawContent(Graphics g){
        g.setColor(Color.RED); // set fill color to red
        g.fillRect(x, y, width, height);
        g.setColor(Color.BLACK); // restore the color to black
    }
}
```

Canvas.java in package com.template.cases;

```java
import java.awt.*;
import java.awt.event.*;
import java.awt.image.BufferedImage;
import java.io.*;
import java.util.*;
import javax.imageio.ImageIO;
import javax.swing.*;

public class Canvas extends JPanel {
    private Rectangle rectange1;
    private Rectangle rectange2;

    public Canvas() {
        this.setLayout(null);
        this.setBackground(Color.WHITE);
        this.requestFocus();

        rectange1= new GreenRectangle(50, 50, 100,50);
        rectange2= new RedRectangle(50, 120, 100,50);
    }

    protected void paintComponent(Graphics g) {
        super.paintComponent(g);

        rectange1.draw(g);
        rectange2.draw(g);
    }
}
```

2. Create a Test class: Test.java **in package** com.template.cases;

```java
import java.awt.*;
import javax.swing.*;

public class Test {
    private static Canvas canvas;

    public static void main(String[] args) {
        JFrame frame = new JFrame("Test Template Method Pattern Case");
        canvas = new Canvas();
        frame.add(canvas);
        frame.setSize(300, 300);
        frame.setVisible(true);
        canvas.requestFocus();
    }
}
```

Right click Test.java, **and then** Run As –> Java Application **Result:**

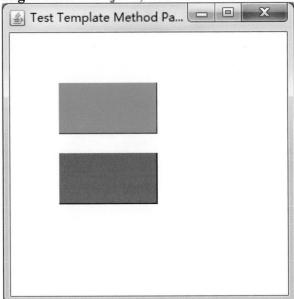

Factory Pattern Principle

Factory Pattern: Provides an interface for creating objects in a superclass, but let subclasses decide which class to instantiate.

1. Example: Products can be created by the factory

Analysis:
1. Create a interface: Product.
2. Create a public method print() to print message.
3. Create a Factory class and then static method: Product create(**String** type).
4. If type equal "computer" then create a instance of Computer.
   If type equal "mouse" then create a instance of Mouse.

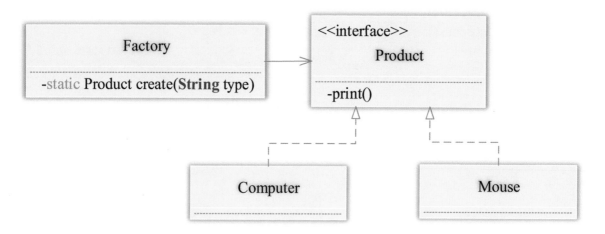

Product.java in package com.factory.principle;

```
public interface Product {

    public void print();
}
```

Computer.java in package com.factory.principle;

```java
public class Computer implements Product{

   public void print() {
      System.out.println("Dell Computer");
   }
}
```

Mouse.java in package com.factory.principle;

```java
public class Mouse implements Product{

   public void print() {
      System.out.println("IBM Mouse");
   }
}
```

Factory.java in package com.factory.principle;

```java
public class Factory {

   public static Product create(String type) {
      Product p = null;
      if ("computer".equals(type)) {
         p = new Computer();
      } else if ("mouse".equals(type)) {
         p = new Mouse();
      }
      return p;
   }
}
```

2. Create a Test class : TestFactory.java in package com.factory.principle;

```java
public class TestFactory {

    public static void main(String[] args) {
        Product p = Factory.create("computer");
        p.print();

        p = Factory.create("mouse");
        p.print();
    }
}
```

Right click TestFactory.java, and then Run As –> Java Application Result:

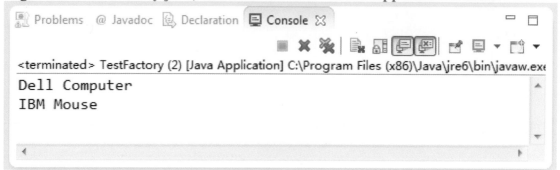

```
Problems   @ Javadoc   Declaration   Console ✕

<terminated> TestFactory (2) [Java Application] C:\Program Files (x86)\Java\jre6\bin\javaw.exe
Dell Computer
IBM Mouse
```

Advantage:
Users only need to know the name of product to get the instance of product they want, without knowing the specific creation process of the product.

Class can be instantiated by String name. let us use real examples to explain this advantage in next chapter.

Factory Pattern Case

1. Example :

Create and instantiate objects by reading the bean.xml file. read the bean.xml file, get the class="**com.factory.cases.UserSQLDAO**" through id="**userDAO**", and then instantiate it through reflection.

```xml
<?xml version="1.0" encoding="UTF-8"?>
<beans>
    <bean id="userDAO"  class="com.factory.cases.UserSQLDAO" />
</beans>
```

Analysis:

1. Create a interface: UserDAO, and then create abstract method: List<User> find() to get all users.
2. Create an implementation class: UserSQLDAO get all users by sql.
3. Create an implementation class: UserProcedureDAO get all users by Stored Procedure.
4. Create a factory class: BeanFactory , and then create method: getBean(String id) to read the bean.xml file, get the class="**com.factory.cases.UserSQLDAO**" through id="**userDAO**", and then instantiate it through reflection.

If the requirements changed, we only need to replace the attribute of class of bean.xml to class="**com.factory.cases.UserProcedureDAO**" without changing other things.

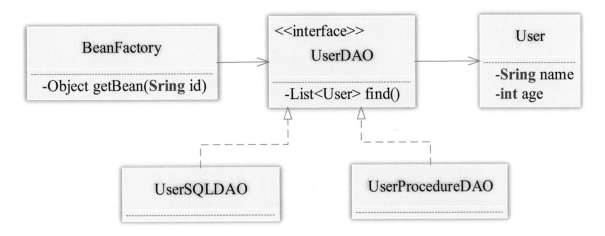

Create a file: bean.xml in project test/src

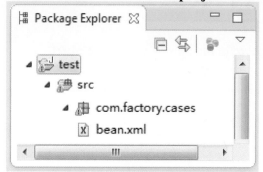

```xml
<?xml version="1.0" encoding="UTF-8"?>
<beans>
    <bean id="userDAO"  class="com.factory.cases.UserSQLDAO" />
</beans>
```

Download the jar package for parsing XML
dom4j-1.6.1.jar
jaxen-1.1-beta-6.jar

http://en.verejava.com/download.jsp?id=1

Create folder: lib and then copy dom4j-1.6.1.jar , jaxen-1.1-beta-6.jar **to the lib**

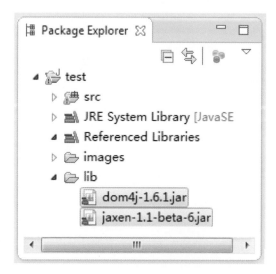

Add dom4j-1.6.1.jar , jaxen-1.1-beta-6.jar **to Referenced Libraries that we can import.**

Select dom4j-1.6.1.jar , jaxen-1.1-beta-6.jar
and then Right click -> Build Path -> Add to Build Path

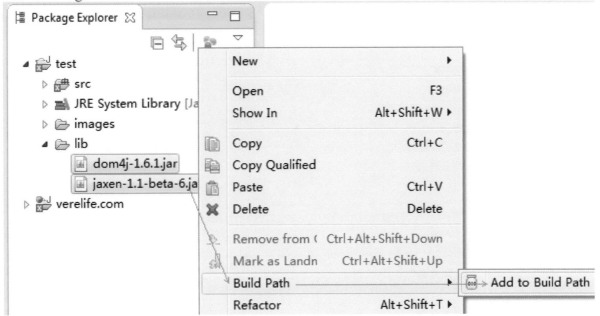

We can see dom4j-1.6.1.jar , jaxen-1.1-beta-6.jar **in Referenced Libraries.**

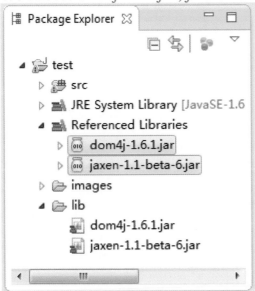

Create all class in package: com.factory.cases

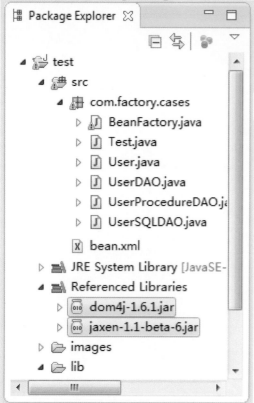

User.java in package com.factory.cases;

```java
public class User {
    private String name;
    private int age;

    public User(String name, int age) {
        this.name = name;
        this.age = age;
    }

    public String getName() {
        return name;
    }

    public int getAge() {
        return age;
    }
}
```

UserDAO.java in package com.factory.cases;

```java
import java.util.List;

public interface UserDAO {

    public List<User> find();
}
```

UserSQLDAO.java in package com.factory.cases;

```java
import java.util.*;

public class UserSQLDAO implements UserDAO {

    public List<User> find() {
        //We assume get users by sql = "select * from users" return List<User>
        List<User> userList = new ArrayList<User>();
        userList.add(new User("Joseph", 20));
        userList.add(new User("James", 30));

        return userList;
    }
}
```

UserProcedureDAO.java in package com.factory.cases;

```java
import java.util.*;

public class UserProcedureDAO implements UserDAO {

    public List<User> find() {
        //We assume get all users by stored procedure
        List<User> userList = new ArrayList<User>();
        userList.add(new User("David", 40));
        userList.add(new User("Grace", 25));

        return userList;
    }
}
```

BeanFactory.java in package com.factory.cases;

```java
import java.io.*;
import java.util.*;
import org.dom4j.*;
import org.dom4j.io.SAXReader;

public class BeanFactory {

    public static Object getBean(String id) {
        InputStream is = null;
        Object obj = null;
        try {
            SAXReader reader = new SAXReader();
            Object objRef = new Object();
            // get the absolute path of bean.xml
            String absolutePath = objRef.getClass().getResource("/").getPath() + "/bean.xml";
            is = new FileInputStream(absolutePath); // read bean.xml
            Document doc = reader.read(is); // convert bean.xml to Document

            // read all <bean> tag to List<Element>
            List<Element> elementList = doc.selectNodes("/beans/bean");
            for (Element element : elementList) {
                String elementId = element.attributeValue("id"); // get value of id
                String elementClass = element.attributeValue("class"); // get value of class
                if(elementId.equals(id)){
                    Class clazz = Class.forName(elementClass);
                    obj = clazz.newInstance(); // Instantiate object through reflection
                }
            }
        } catch (Exception e) {
            e.printStackTrace();
        } finally {
            try {
                is.close();
            } catch (IOException e) {
                e.printStackTrace();
            }
        }
        return obj;
    }
}
```

2. Create a Test class : Test.java in package com.factory.cases;

```java
import java.util.List;
public class Test {
   public static void main(String[] args) {
      UserDAO userDao = (UserDAO)BeanFactory.getBean("userDAO");

      List<User> userList = userDao.find();
      for(User item: userList){
         System.out.println(item.getName()+" , "+item.getAge());
      }
   }
}
```

Right click Test.java, and then Run As –> Java Application Result:

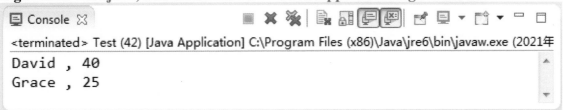

Console ✕

\<terminated\> Test (42) [Java Application] C:\Program Files (x86)\Java\jre6\bin\javaw.exe (2021年
```
Joseph , 20
James , 30
```

We change bean.xml attribute to class="com.factory.cases.UserProcedureDAO"

```xml
<?xml version="1.0" encoding="UTF-8"?>
<beans>
   <bean id="userDAO"  class="com.factory.cases.UserProcedureDAO" />
</beans>
```

Right click Test.java, and then Run As –> Java Application Again Result:

Console ✕

\<terminated\> Test (42) [Java Application] C:\Program Files (x86)\Java\jre6\bin\javaw.exe (2021年
```
David , 40
Grace , 25
```

We only need to replace the attribute value of class of bean.xml to achieve the extended function.

Command Pattern Principle

Command Pattern :
Encapsulate a request as an object, allowing you to parameterize different requests.

1. Example: The mouse click Ok or Cancel Button will trigger the click event

Analysis:
1. Create 1 class: ActionEvent that encapsulates the source of the event.
2. Create 1 interface: ActionListener that is notified whenever you click on the button
3. Create 1 class: Button and then create a method: addActionListener(ActionListener l) that add the specified action listener to receive action events
4. Create 1 class: Mouse and then create a method: click(Button btn) that simulate mouse click button

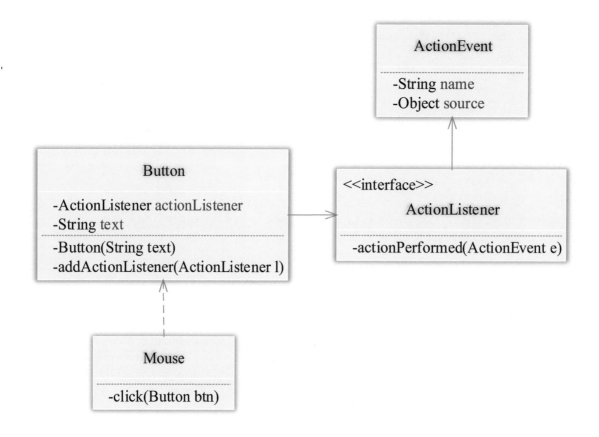

ActionListener.java in package com.command.principle;

```java
public interface ActionListener {

    public void actionPerformed(ActionEvent e);
}
```

ActionEvent.java in package com.command.principle;

```java
public class ActionEvent {
    private String name;
    private Object source;

    public ActionEvent(String name, Object source) {
        super();
        this.name = name;
        this.source = source;
    }

    public String getName() {
        return name;
    }

    public void setName(String name) {
        this.name = name;
    }

    public Object getSource() {
        return source;
    }

    public void setSource(Object source) {
        this.source = source;
    }
}
```

Button.java **in package com.command.principle;**

```java
public class Button {
  private ActionListener actionListener;
  private String text;

  public Button(String text) {
    super();
    this.text = text;
  }

  public ActionListener getActionListener() {
    return actionListener;
  }

  public void addActionListener(ActionListener actionListener) {
    this.actionListener = actionListener;
  }

  public String getText() {
    return text;
  }

  public void setText(String text) {
    this.text = text;
  }
}
```

Mouse.java **in package com.command.principle;**

```java
public class Mouse {

  public void click(Button btn) {
    ActionEvent e = new ActionEvent(btn.getText(), btn);
    btn.getActionListener().actionPerformed(e);
  }
}
```

3. Create a Test class : TestCommand.java in package com.command.principle;

```java
import java.util.ArrayList;
public class TestCommand {

    public static void main(String[] args) {
        Button btnOk = new Button("Ok");
        Button btnCancel = new Button("Cancel");

        btnOk.addActionListener(new ActionListener() { //Add a listen event
            @Override
            public void actionPerformed(ActionEvent e) {
                System.out.println("OK button is clicked");
            }
        });

        btnCancel.addActionListener(new ActionListener() {//Add a listen event
            @Override
            public void actionPerformed(ActionEvent e) {
                System.out.println("Cancel button is clicked");
            }
        });

        Mouse m = new Mouse();
        m.click(btnOk); //Mouse click OK button
        m.click(btnCancel);//Mouse click Cancel button
    }
}
```

Right click TestCommand.java, and then Run As –> Java Application Result:

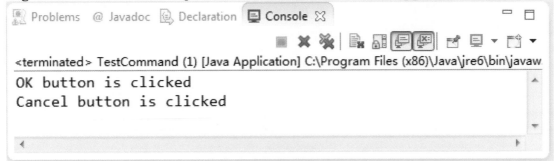

79

Command Pattern Case

1. Example: Use Java Swing GUI to create a chat room window, click the close button to close the dialog box, click the send button to add the message to the Chat Box

Analysis:

1. Create 1 class: ChatFrame inherit from JFrame.

2. Add message box(JTextField txtMessage), chat box(JTextArea txtChat), send button(JButton btnSend) and close button(JButton btnClose) on ChatFrame. click the close button to close the ChatFrame, click the send button to add the message to the chat box

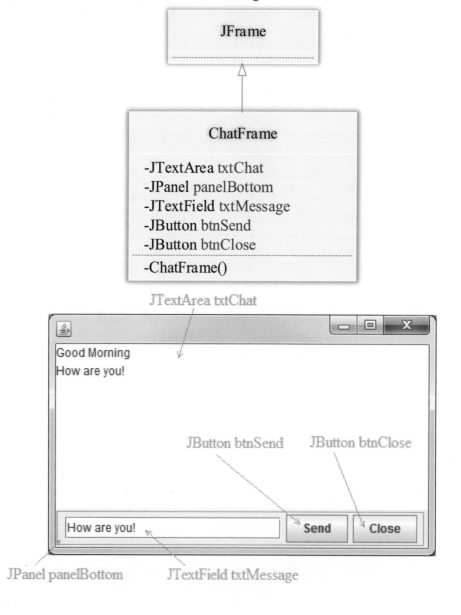

ChatFrame.java in package com.command.cases;

```java
import java.awt.*;
import java.awt.event.*;
import javax.swing.*;
public class ChatFrame extends JFrame {
    private JTextArea txtChat;
    private JPanel panelBottom;
    private JTextField txtMessage;
    private JButton btnSend;
    private JButton btnClose;

    public ChatFrame(){
        this.setSize(400,300);
        this.add(getTxtChat(),BorderLayout.CENTER);
        this.add(getPanelBottom(), BorderLayout.SOUTH);

        this.setVisible(true);
    }

    public JTextArea getTxtChat() {
        if(txtChat == null){
            txtChat = new JTextArea();
        }
        return txtChat;
    }

    public JPanel getPanelBottom() {
        if(panelBottom == null){
            panelBottom = new JPanel();
            panelBottom.add(getTxtMessage());
            panelBottom.add(getBtnSend());
            panelBottom.add(getBtnClose());
        }
        return panelBottom;
    }

    public JTextField getTxtMessage() {
        if(txtMessage == null){
            txtMessage = new JTextField();
            txtMessage.setColumns(20);
        }
        return txtMessage;
    }
```

```java
    public JButton getBtnSend() {
        if(btnSend == null){
            btnSend = new JButton("Send");
            btnSend.addActionListener(new ActionListener(){
                public void actionPerformed(ActionEvent e) {
                    txtChat.append(txtMessage.getText() + "\n");
                }

            });
        }
        return btnSend;
    }

    public JButton getBtnClose() {
        if(btnClose == null){
            btnClose = new JButton("Close");
            btnClose.addActionListener(new ActionListener(){
                public void actionPerformed(ActionEvent e) {
                    System.exit(-1);
                }

            });
        }
        return btnClose;
    }
}
```

2. Create a Test class : Test.java in package com.command.cases;

```java
import java.awt.*;
import javax.swing.*;
public class Test {
    public static void main(String[] args) {
        ChatFrame frame = new ChatFrame();
    }
}
```

Right click Test.java, and then Run As –> Java Application will see the chat dialog.

Builder Pattern Principle

Builder Pattern: Separate the construction of a complex object from its representation so that the same construction processes can create different representations.

1. Example: Car divided into three parts: head, body, wheel. build different kinds of car according to different requirement.

Analysis:
1. Create a interface: Builder, and then create 3 method: buildHead(), buildBody(), buildWheel(). finally, assemble car through method: Car buildPart().
2. Create an implementation class: StandardBuilder to build honda car.
3. Create an implementation class: AdvancedBuilder to build Mercedes-Benz car.

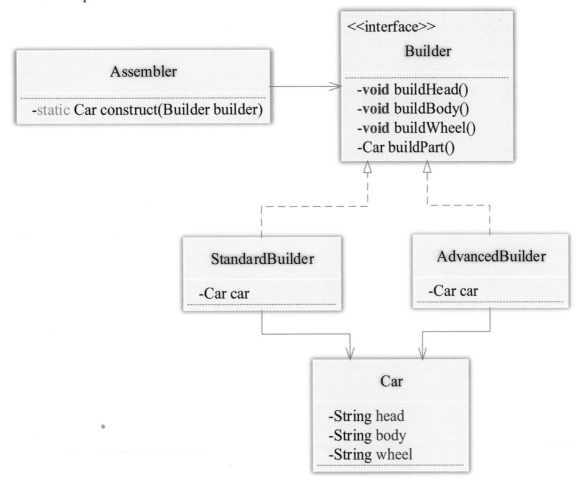

Car.java in package com.builder.principle;

```java
public class Car {
    private String head;
    private String body;
    private String wheel;

    public String getHead() {
        return head;
    }

    public void setHead(String head) {
        this.head = head;
    }

    public String getBody() {
        return body;
    }

    public void setBody(String body) {
        this.body = body;
    }

    public String getWheel() {
        return wheel;
    }

    public void setWheel(String wheel) {
        this.wheel = wheel;
    }
}
```

Builder.java in package com.builder.principle;

```java
public interface Builder {

    public void buildHead();

    public void buildBody();

    public void buildWheel();

    public Car buildPart();
}
```

StandardBuilder.java in package com.builder.principle;

```java
public class StandardBuilder implements Builder {
    Car car = null;

    public StandardBuilder() {
        car = new Car();
    }

    public void buildHead() {
        car.setHead("Honda's head has been completed");
    }

    public void buildBody() {
        car.setBody("Honda's body has been completed");
    }

    public void buildWheel() {
        car.setWheel("Honda's wheel has been completed");
    }

    public Car buildPart() {
        return car;
    }
}
```

AdvancedBuilder.java in package com.builder.principle;

```java
public class AdvancedBuilder implements Builder {
    Car car = null;

    public AdvancedBuilder() {
        car = new Car();
    }

    public void buildHead() {
        car.setHead("Mercedes-Benz's head has been completed");
    }

    public void buildBody() {
        car.setBody("Mercedes-Benz's body has been completed");
    }

    public void buildWheel() {
        car.setWheel("Mercedes-Benz's wheel has been completed");
    }

    public Car buildPart() {
        return car;
    }
}
```

Assembler.java in package com.builder.principle;

```java
public class Assembler {

    public static Car construct(Builder builder) {

        builder.buildHead();
        builder.buildBody();
        builder.buildWheel();
        return builder.buildPart();
    }
}
```

2. Create a Test class : TestBuilder.java in package com.builder.principle;

```java
public class TestBuilder {

    public static void main(String[] args) {

        Car hondaCar = Assembler.construct(new StandardBuilder());
        System.out.println(hondaCar.getHead());
        System.out.println(hondaCar.getBody());
        System.out.println(hondaCar.getWheel());

        System.out.println("----------------------");

        Car benzCar = Assembler.construct(new AdvancedBuilder());
        System.out.println(benzCar.getHead());
        System.out.println(benzCar.getBody());
        System.out.println(benzCar.getWheel());

    }
}
```

Right click TestBuilder.java, and then Run As –> Java Application Result:

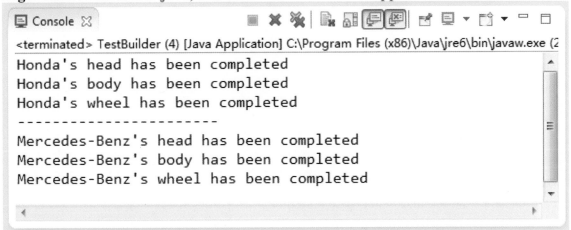

```
Console
<terminated> TestBuilder (4) [Java Application] C:\Program Files (x86)\Java\jre6\bin\javaw.exe (2
Honda's head has been completed
Honda's body has been completed
Honda's wheel has been completed
----------------------
Mercedes-Benz's head has been completed
Mercedes-Benz's body has been completed
Mercedes-Benz's wheel has been completed
```

The builder pattern advantages:
1. Good encapsulation, the client does not need to know the implementation details of internal products.
2. The builder is independent and easy to expand.

Builder Pattern Case

1. Example: Builder custom dialog according to different requirement.

Analysis:

1. Create a class: Dialog inherit from JFrame and then create 4 method: setTitle(String title), setContent(Component content), setOkButton(JButton okButton), setCloseButton(JButton closeButton)

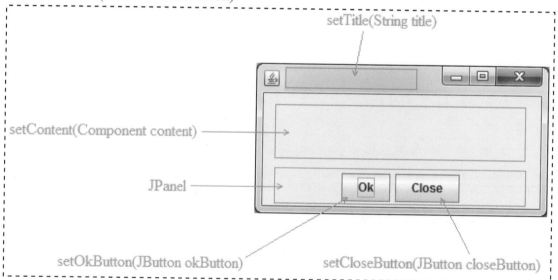

2. Create a interface: Builder, and then create 4 method: buildTitle(String title), buildContent(String message), buildOkButton(String name, ActionListener listener), buildCloseButton(String name, ActionListener listener). finally, create Dialog through method: Dialog create().

3. Create an implementation class: MessasgeBuilder to build message dailog.

UML Diagram:

```
<<interface>>
Builder
---------------------------------------------
-buildTitle(String title)
-buildContent(String message)
-buildOkButton(String name, ActionListener listener)
-buildCloseButton(String name, ActionListener listener)
-Dialog create()
```

```
MessageBuilder
---------------------------------------------
-Dialog dialog
---------------------------------------------
-public MessageBuilder()
-buildTitle(String title)
-buildContent(String message)
-buildCloseButton(String name,ActionListener listener)
-Dialog create()
```

```
Dialog
---------------------------------------------
-JPanel bottomPanel
---------------------------------------------
-public Dialog()
-setTitle(String title)
-setContent(Component content)
-setOkButton(JButton okButton)
-setCloseButton(JButton closeButton)
```

```
JFrame
---------------------------------------------
```

Create all classes in project test/com.builder.cases

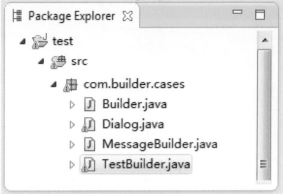

Dialog.java **in package** com.builder.cases;

```java
import java.awt.*;
import javax.swing.*;
public class Dialog extends JFrame{
  private JPanel bottomPanel;

  public Dialog(){
    this.setSize(300, 150);
    this.setLayout(new BorderLayout());
    bottomPanel = new JPanel();
    this.add(bottomPanel,BorderLayout.SOUTH);
  }

  public void setTitle(String title) {
    super.setTitle(title);
  }

  public void setContent(Component content) {
    this.add(content, BorderLayout.CENTER);
  }

  public void setOkButton(JButton okButton) {
    bottomPanel.add(okButton);
  }

  public void setCloseButton(JButton closeButton) {
    bottomPanel.add(closeButton);
  }
}
```

Builder.java in package com.builder.cases;

```java
import java.awt.event.ActionListener;
public interface Builder {

    public void buildTitle(String title);
    public void buildContent(String message);
    public void buildOkButton(String name, ActionListener listener);
    public void buildCloseButton(String name, ActionListener listener);
    public Dialog create();
}
```

MessageBuilder.java in package com.builder.cases;

```java
import java.awt.event.ActionListener;
import javax.swing.*;
public class MessageBuilder implements Builder {
    Dialog dialog = null;

    public MessageBuilder() {
        dialog = new Dialog();
    }

    public void buildTitle(String title){
        dialog.setTitle(title);
    }

    public void buildContent(String message){
        dialog.setContent(new JLabel(message));
    }

    public void buildOkButton(String name, ActionListener listener){
        JButton button = new JButton(name);
        button.addActionListener(listener);
        dialog.setOkButton(button);
    }

    public void buildCloseButton(String name,ActionListener listener){
        JButton button = new JButton(name);
        button.addActionListener(listener);
        dialog.setCloseButton(button);
    }
```

```java
  public Dialog create(){
    return dialog;
  }
}
```

2. Create a Test class : TestBuilder.java in package com.builder.cases;

```java
import java.awt.event.*;
import javax.swing.*;

public class TestBuilder {
  static Dialog dialog;

  public static void main(String[] args) {

    Builder builder = new MessageBuilder();
    builder.buildTitle("Message Dialog");
    builder.buildContent("Please input username?");
    builder.buildCloseButton("Close", new ActionListener(){

      public void actionPerformed(ActionEvent e) {
        dialog.dispose();
      }
    });
    dialog = builder.create();
    dialog.show();
  }
}
```

Right click TestBuilder.java, and then Run As –> Java Application Result:

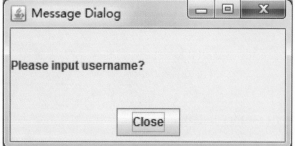

Change the Test class to create confirm message dialog :

```java
import java.awt.event.*;
import javax.swing.*;

public class TestBuilder {
    static Dialog dialog;

    public static void main(String[] args) {

        Builder builder = new MessageBuilder();
        builder.buildTitle("Confirm Dialog");
        builder.buildContent("Do you want to delete this product ?");

        builder.buildOkButton("Ok", new ActionListener(){
            public void actionPerformed(ActionEvent e) {

            }
        });

        builder.buildCloseButton("Close", new ActionListener(){
            public void actionPerformed(ActionEvent e) {
                dialog.dispose();
            }
        });
        dialog = builder.create();
        dialog.show();
    }
}
```

Right click Test.java, and then Run As –> Java Application Result:

Adapter Pattern Principle

Adapter Pattern: Convert the interface of a class into another interface clients expect. Adapter lets classes work together with incompatible interfaces.

1. Example: The original power is 120 voltages, and it needs to be adapted to 12 voltages for computer.

Analysis:
1. Create a interface: Plug, and then create a method: recharge().
2. Create an implementation class: StandardPlug can recharge 120 V.
3. Create an Adapter class: AdapterPlug can convert StandardPlug recharge 12 V for computer.

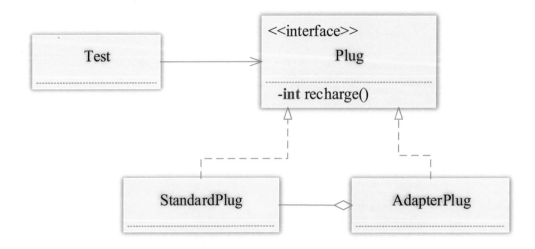

Plug.java in package com.adapter.principle;

```java
public interface Plug {

   public int recharge();
}
```

StandardPlug.java in package com.adapter.principle;

```java
public class StandardPlug implements Plug{

   public int recharge() {
      return 120; //Power is 120 Voltage
   }
}
```

AdapterPlug.java in package com.adapter.principle;

```java
public class AdapterPlug implements Plug {

   public int recharge() {
      Plug plug = new StandardPlug();
      int v = plug.recharge();
      v = v - 108;
      return v;
   }
}
```

2. Create a Test class : Test.java in package com.adapter.principle;

```java
public class Test {

    public static void main(String[] args) {
        Plug plug = new StandardPlug();
        System.out.println(plug.recharge() + " too much voltage");

        plug = new AdapterPlug();
        System.out.println("Adapter convert into " + plug.recharge() + " voltage.");
    }
}
```

Right click Test.java, and then Run As –> Java Application Result:

```
Console ☒                    ■ ✖ ✖ | ▤ ▥ ▣ ▣ | ▱ ▯ ▾ ▭ ▾ ⚊ ⊟
<terminated> Test (43) [Java Application] C:\Program Files (x86)\Java\jre6\bin\javaw.exe (2021年
120 too much voltage
Adapter convert into 12 voltage
```

Adapter Pattern Case

Example: Draw Text List Menu and Image List Menu on Canvas:

Read data from xml, the same data but different adapter show different view.

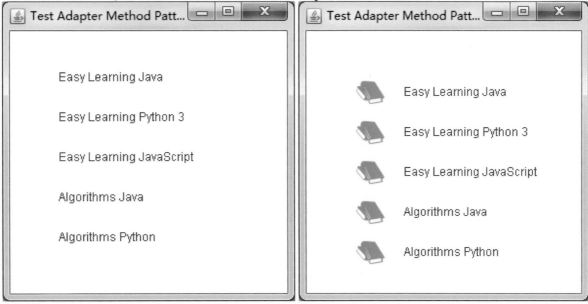

Analysis:

1. Create a interface: Adapter, and then create a method: List createMenu().
2. Create an implementation class: TextAdapter can create a text list from xml.
3. Create an Adapter class: ImageAdapter can convert TextAdapter to image list.

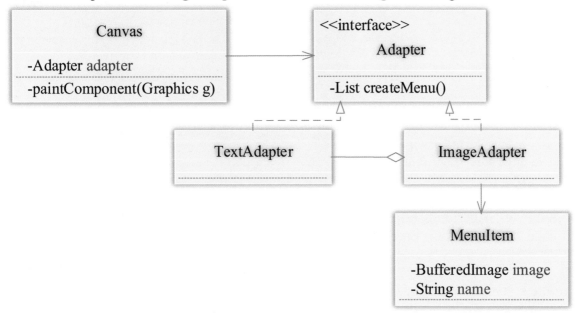

Create all classes in project test/com.adapter.cases

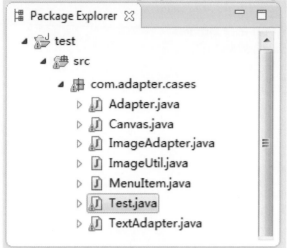

Adapter.java **in package** com.adapter.cases;

```java
import java.util.List;
public interface Adapter {

    public List createMenu();
}
```

TextAdapter.java **in package** com.adapter.cases;

```java
import java.util.*;
public class TextAdapter implements Adapter {
    private List data;

    public TextAdapter(String xml) {
        // For example, these data come from reading xml
        data = new ArrayList();
        data.add("Easy Learning Java");
        data.add("Easy Learning Python 3");
        data.add("Easy Learning JavaScript");
        data.add("Algorithms Java");
        data.add("Algorithms Python");
    }

    public List createMenu() {
        return this.data;
    }
}
```

Canvas.java in package com.adapter.cases;

```java
import java.awt.Color;
import java.awt.Graphics;
import java.util.List;
import javax.swing.JPanel;

public class Canvas extends JPanel {
    Adapter adapter;

    public Canvas() {
        this.setLayout(null);
        this.setBackground(Color.WHITE);
        this.requestFocus();

        String xml = "menu.xml";
        adapter = new TextAdapter(xml);
    }

    protected void paintComponent(Graphics g) {
        super.paintComponent(g);

        List data = adapter.createMenu();
        int x = 50;
        int y = 50;
        for (int i = 0; i<data.size();i++) {
            String menuName = data.get(i).toString();
            g.drawString(menuName, x, y); // draw menu name
            y += 40; //the y coordinate moves down 40 pixels for drawing next menu
        }
    }
}
```

2. Create a Test class: Test.java in package com.adapter.cases;

```java
import java.awt.*;
import javax.swing.*;

public class Test {
    private static Canvas canvas;

    public static void main(String[] args) {
        JFrame frame = new JFrame("Test Adapter Pattern Case");
        canvas = new Canvas();
        frame.add(canvas);
        frame.setSize(300, 300);
        frame.setVisible(true);
        canvas.requestFocus();
    }
}
```

Right click Test.java, and then Run As –> Java Application Result:

3. If there is a new requirement that basis on the original data, not only the original text list remain unchanged, but also the image list menu must be implemented in the new system. We can creaete a ImageAdapter to convert the original data to an image list

Copy book.png to test/icon

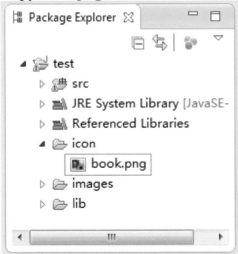

Copy ImageUtil.java code here from the previous chapter: Animation

MenuItem.java in package com.adapter.cases;

```java
import java.awt.image.BufferedImage;
public class MenuItem {
    private BufferedImage image;
    private String name;

    public MenuItem(String imagePath, String name) {
        this.image = ImageUtil.loadImage(imagePath);
        this.name = name;
    }

    public BufferedImage getImage() {
        return image;
    }

    public String getName() {
        return name;
    }
}
```

ImageAdapter.java in package com.adapter.cases;

```java
import java.util.*;

public class ImageAdapter implements Adapter {

    private List data;

    public ImageAdapter(String xml) {
        TextAdapter adapter = new TextAdapter(xml);
        List adapterList = adapter.createMenu();

        // convert original data to image list  List<MenuItem>
        data = new ArrayList();
        for(int i =0; i <adapterList.size(); i++){
            String name = adapterList.get(i).toString();
            data.add(new MenuItem("icon/book.png", name));
        }
    }

    public List createMenu() {

        return this.data;
    }
}
```

Canvas.java in package com.adapter.cases;

```java
import java.awt.Color;
import java.awt.Graphics;
import java.util.List;
import javax.swing.JPanel;
public class Canvas extends JPanel {
    Adapter adapter;

    public Canvas() {
        this.setLayout(null);
        this.setBackground(Color.WHITE);
        this.requestFocus();

        String xml = "menu.xml";
        adapter = new ImageAdapter(xml);
    }
```

```
protected void paintComponent(Graphics g) {
  super.paintComponent(g);

  List data = adapter.createMenu();
  int x = 50;
  int y = 50;
  for (int i = 0; i<data.size();i++) {
    MenuItem menuItem = (MenuItem)data.get(i);
    g.drawImage(menuItem.getImage(), x , y, null); // draw image
    g.drawString(menuItem.getName(), x + 50, y + 15); // draw menu name
    y += 40;
  }
 }
}
```

Right click Test.java, and then Run As –> Java Application Result:

Facade Pattern Principle

Facade Pattern: A single class that represents an entire subsystem. Provide a unified interface to a set of interfaces in a system. Facade defines a higher-level interface that makes the subsystem easier to use.

1. Example:

Stage provide a consistent interface to perform : light, music and video.

Analysis:

1. Create 3 interface: Light, Music, Video and then create the method: flash(),play(),show()
2. Create 3 implementation class: LightImpl, MusicImpl, VideoImpl.
3. Create a Facade class: Facade. Facade communicates with client.

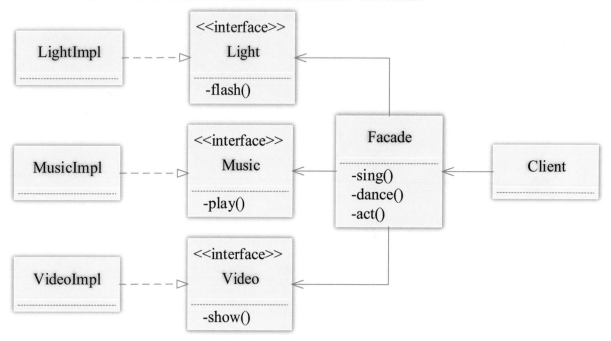

Light.java in package com.facade.principle;

```java
public interface Light {

    public void flash();
}
```

LightImpl.java in package com.facade.principle;

```java
public class LightImpl implements Light {

    public void flash() {
        System.out.println("Starting color flash");
    }
}
```

Music.java in package com.facade.principle;

```java
public interface Music {

    public void play();
}
```

MusicImpl.java in package com.facade.principle;

```java
public class MusicImpl implements Music {

    public void play() {
        System.out.println("Playing classical music");
    }
}
```

Video.java in package com.facade.principle;

```java
public interface Video {

    public void show();
}
```

VideoImpl.java in package com.facade.principle;

```java
public class VideoImpl implements Video {

    public void show() {
        System.out.println("Show video");
    }
}
```

Facade.java in package com.facade.principle;

```java
//provides a consistent interface to call
public class Facade {
    private Light light;
    private Music music;
    private Video video;

    public Facade() {
        light = new LightImpl();
        music = new MusicImpl();
        video = new VideoImpl();
    }

    public void sing() {
        System.out.println("Start singing with ");
        light.flash();
        music.play();
    }

    public void dance() {
        System.out.println("Start dancing with ");
        light.flash();
        music.play();
        video.show();
    }

    public void act() {
        System.out.println("Start acting with ");
        light.flash();
        video.show();
    }
}
```

2. Create a Test class : TestClient.java in package com.facade.principle;

```java
public class TestClient {

  public static void main(String[] args) {
    Facade facade = new Facade();

    facade.sing();

    System.out.println("-----------------------------");

    facade.dance();

    System.out.println("-----------------------------");

    facade.act();
  }
}
```

Right click TestClient.java, and then Run As –> Java Application Result:

```
Console ☒                    ■ ✖ ✖  ⬛ ⬛ 🔲 🔲  🔲 🖥 ▾ 🔲 ▾ ▭ 🔲
<terminated> TestFacade (2) [Java Application] C:\Program Files (x86)\Java\jre6\bin\javaw.exe (20
Start singing with                                                  ▲
Starting color flash
Playing classical music
-----------------------------
Start dancing with
Starting color flash
Playing classical music
Show video                                                          ≡
-----------------------------
Start acting with
Starting color flash
Show video                                                          ▼
◀                                                                  ▶
```

Facade Pattern Case

Example: DBUtil class encapsulates JDBC that provide consistent interface for the client to access the database

If you want to learn JDBC + MySQL or Oracle please read book

<<Easy Learning JDBC + MySQL>>
<<Easy Learning MySQL SQL>>
<<Easy Learning JDBC + Oracle>>
<<Easy Learning Oracle SQL>>

http://en.verejava.com

Analysis:
1. The Java Database Connectivity (JDBC) API provides universal data access from the Java programming language. Using the JDBC API, you can access virtually any data source: Oracle MySQL MSSQL,Spread Sheets etc. JDBC technology also provides a common base on which tools and alternate interfaces can be built.
2. The Commons DBUtil is a small set of classes designed to work with JDBC easier to query and update data.

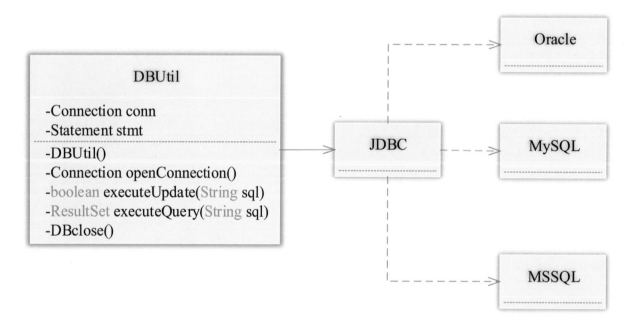

1. Download mysql driver jar to connect mysql database.

mysql-connector-java-5.1.45-bin.jar

http://en.verejava.com/download.jsp?id=1

2. Open cmd console and login to MySQL with your username/password and then create a database : test

Mysql -uroot -p19810109

create database test;

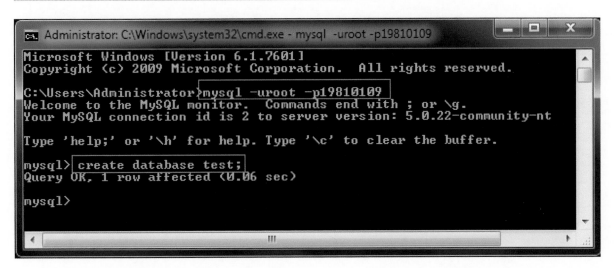

3. Open database test and then create a table: users

uses test;

create table users
(
   id **int primary key** auto_increment,
   username **varchar(**100**)**,
   pwd **varchar(**100**)**
);

```
mysql> use test;
Database changed
mysql> create table users
    -> (
    ->      id int primary key auto_increment,
    ->      username varchar(100),
    ->      pwd varchar(100)
    -> );
Query OK, 0 rows affected (0.06 sec)

mysql> desc users;
+----------+--------------+------+-----+---------+----------------+
| Field    | Type         | Null | Key | Default | Extra          |
+----------+--------------+------+-----+---------+----------------+
| id       | int(11)      | NO   | PRI | NULL    | auto_increment |
| username | varchar(100) | YES  |     | NULL    |                |
| pwd      | varchar(100) | YES  |     | NULL    |                |
+----------+--------------+------+-----+---------+----------------+
3 rows in set (0.06 sec)

mysql>
```

4. Copy and add mysql-connector-java-5.1.45-bin.jar **to project** test

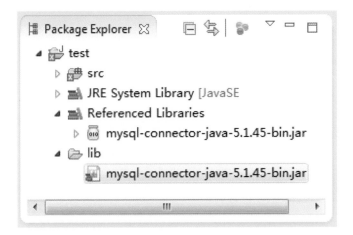

DBUtil.java in package com.facade.cases;

```java
import java.sql.*;
import java.util.Date;

public class DBUtil {
    protected Connection conn;
    protected Statement stmt;

    public DBUtil() {
        try {
            Class.forName("com.mysql.jdbc.Driver"); //Load jdbc driver
        } catch (ClassNotFoundException e) {
            e.printStackTrace();
        }
    }

    //Open Database Connection
    public Connection openConnection() {
        try {
            return
DriverManager.getConnection("jdbc:mysql://localhost/test?useUnicode=true&characterEncod
ing=utf-8", "root", "19810109");
        } catch (SQLException e) {
            e.printStackTrace();
        }
        return null;
    }
```

```java
public boolean executeUpdate(String sql) {  //execute add delete update sql
   conn = openConnection();
   try {
      Statement stmt = conn.createStatement();
      if (stmt.executeUpdate(sql) > 0) {
         return true;
      }
   } catch (SQLException e) {
      e.printStackTrace();
   } finally {
      if (conn != null) {
         try {
            conn.close();
         } catch (SQLException e) {
            e.printStackTrace();
         }
      }
   }
   return false;
}

public ResultSet executeQuery(String sql) { //execute query sql
   conn = openConnection();
   try {
      Statement stmt = conn.createStatement();
      return stmt.executeQuery(sql);
   } catch (SQLException e) {
      e.printStackTrace();
   }
   return null;
}

public void DBClose() {
   if (conn != null) {
      try {
         conn.close();
      } catch (SQLException e) {
         e.printStackTrace();
      }
   }
}
}
```

Create a test class: TestAdd.java in package com.facade.cases;

```java
public class TestAdd {

    public static void main(String[] args) {
        //Add User
        DBUtil db = new DBUtil();
        String sql = "insert into users(username,pwd)values('david','444444')";
        db.executeUpdate(sql);
    }
}
```

**Right click TestAdd.java and then Run as -> Java Application
and then see the result in mysql:**

Create a test class: TestUpdate.java **in package** com.facade.cases;

```java
public class TestUpdate {

  public static void main(String[] args) {

    //Update User
    DBUtil db = new DBUtil();
    String sql = "update users set pwd='555555' where username='david'";
    db.executeUpdate(sql);
  }
}
```

Right click TestUpdate.java **and then** Run as -> Java Application
and then see the result in mysql:

Create a test class: TestQuery.java in package com.facade.cases;

```java
import java.sql.*;

public class TestQuery {

    public static void main(String[] args) {

        //Query from users
        DBUtil db = new DBUtil();
        String sql = "select * from users";
        ResultSet rs = db.executeQuery(sql);
        try {
            while (rs.next()) {
                int id = rs.getInt("id");
                String username = rs.getString("username");
                String pwd = rs.getString("pwd");
                System.out.println(id + "," + username + "," + pwd);
            }
        } catch (SQLException e) {
            e.printStackTrace();
        } finally {
            db.DBClose();
        }
    }
}
```

Right click TestQuery.java and then Run as -> Java Application and then see the result in Eclipse:

Decorator Pattern Principle

Decorator Pattern: Add additional responsibilities to objects dynamically. Decorator provide a flexible alternative to subclassing for extending functionality.

1. Example: Person play different roles in life. They are fathers at home, managers in the company, and actors on stage etc.

Analysis:
1. Create 1 interface: Person and then create the method: showRole() .
2. Create 1 implementation class: Man to show his role is man .
3. Create a abstract decorator class: Decorator.
4. Create 1 implementation class: ManagerDecorator to decorate person as manager.
5. Create 1 implementation class: ActorDecorator to decorate person as Actor.

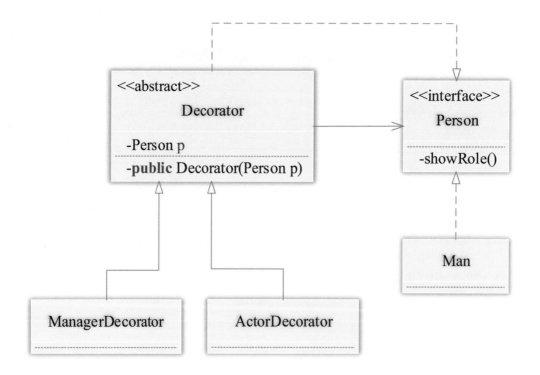

Person.java in package com.decorator.principle;

```java
public interface Person {

    public void showRole();
}
```

Man.java in package com.decorator.principle;

```java
public class Man implements Person {

    public void showRole() {
        System.out.println("I am a man");
    }
}
```

Decorator.java in package com.decorator.principle;

```java
public abstract class Decorator implements Person {
    protected Person p;

    public Decorator(Person p) {
        this.p = p;
    }
}
```

ManagerDecorator.java in package com.decorator.principle;

```java
public class ManagerDecorator extends Decorator {
    public ManagerDecorator(Person p) {
        super(p);
    }

    public void showRole() {
        p.showRole();
        System.out.println("I am still a manager");
    }
}
```

ActorDecorator.java in package com.decorator.principle;

```java
public class ActorDecorator extends Decorator {
    public ActorDecorator(Person p) {
        super(p);
    }

    public void showRole() {
        p.showRole();
        System.out.println("I am still an international actor.");
    }
}
```

2. Create a Test class : TestDecorator.java in package com.decorator.principle;

```java
public class TestDecorator {
    public static void main(String[] args) {
        Person p = new Man();
        p.showRole();

        System.out.println("----------------------");

        p = new ManagerDecorator(p);
        p.showRole();

        System.out.println("----------------------");

        p = new ActorDecorator(p);
        p.showRole();
    }
}
```

Right click TestDecorator.java and then Run as -> Java Application Result:

```
Problems  @ Javadoc  Declaration  Console

I am a man
---------------------------
I am a man
I am still a manager
---------------------------
I am a man
I am still a manager
I am still an international actor.
```

Decorator Pattern Case

1. Example: In the game, the girl can be decorated with different skirts

Analysis:

1. Create 1 interface: Person and then create the method: draw(Graphics g)
2. Create 1 implementation class: Girl to draw image of girl on canvas .
3. Create a abstract decorator class: Decorator.
4. Create 1 implementation class: YellowDecorator to decorate girl with yellow skirt.
5. Create 1 implementation class: BlueDecorator to decorate girl with blue skirt.

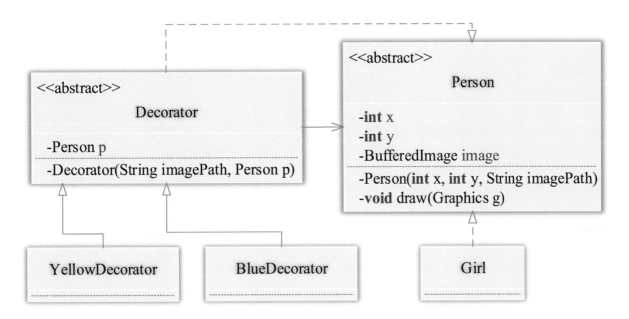

Copy images to test/icon

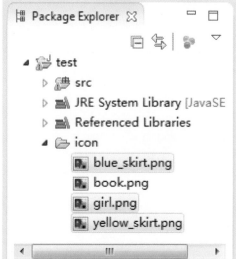

Create all classes in project test/com.decorator.cases

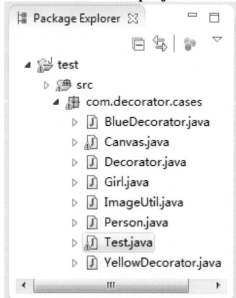

Copy ImageUtil.java code here from the previous chapter: Animation

Person.java in package com.decorator.cases;

```java
import java.awt.Graphics;
import java.awt.image.BufferedImage;

public abstract class Person {
    protected int x;
    protected int y;
    protected BufferedImage image;

    public Person(int x, int y, String imagePath){
        this.x = x;
        this.y = y;
        this.image=ImageUtil.loadImage(imagePath);
    }

    public void draw(Graphics g){
        g.drawImage(image, x, y, null);
    }

    public int getX() {
        return x;
    }

    public int getY() {
        return y;
    }
}
```

Girl.java in package com.decorator.cases;

```java
public class Girl extends Person {

    public Girl(int x, int y, String imagePath) {
        super(x, y, imagePath);
    }
}
```

Decorator.java in package com.decorator.cases;

```java
public abstract class Decorator extends Person {
    protected Person p;

    public Decorator(String imagePath, Person p){
        super(p.getX(), p.getY(), imagePath);
        this.p = p;
    }
}
```

YellowDecorator.java in package com.decorator.cases;

```java
import java.awt.Graphics;

public class YellowDecorator extends Decorator {

    public YellowDecorator(String imagePath, Person p){
        super(imagePath, p);
    }

    public void draw(Graphics g) {
        p.draw(g);

        // draw yellow skirt image on canvas
        x = x + 18;
        y = y + 25;
        g.drawImage(image, x, y, null);
    }
}
```

BlueDecorator.java in package com.decorator.cases;

```java
import java.awt.Graphics;

public class BlueDecorator extends Decorator {

    public BlueDecorator(String imagePath, Person p){
        super(imagePath, p);
    }

    public void draw(Graphics g) {
        p.draw(g);

        // draw blue skirt image on canvas
        x = x + 24;
        y = y + 20;
        g.drawImage(image, x, y, null);
    }
}
```

Canvas.java in package com.decorator.cases;

```java
import java.awt.*;
import java.util.List;
import javax.swing.JPanel;
public class Canvas extends JPanel {
    Person person;

    public Canvas() {
        this.setLayout(null);
        this.setBackground(Color.WHITE);
        this.requestFocus();

        person = new Girl(50,50,"icon/girl.png");
    }

    protected void paintComponent(Graphics g) {
        super.paintComponent(g);

        person.draw(g);
    }
}
```

2. Create a Test class : Test.java in package com.decorator.cases;

```java
import java.awt.*;
import javax.swing.*;

public class Test {
    private static Canvas canvas;

    public static void main(String[] args) {
        JFrame frame = new JFrame("Test Decorator Pattern Case");
        canvas = new Canvas();
        frame.add(canvas);
        frame.setSize(300, 300);
        frame.setVisible(true);
        canvas.requestFocus();
    }
}
```

Right click Test.java and then Run as -> Java Application Result:

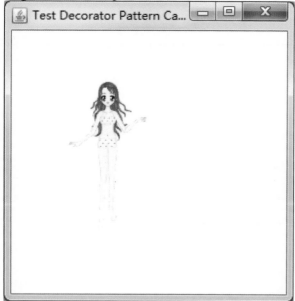

3. Add the code of YellowDecorator in Canvas.java

```java
import java.awt.*;
import java.util.List;
import javax.swing.JPanel;
public class Canvas extends JPanel {
    Person person;

    public Canvas() {
        this.setLayout(null);
        this.setBackground(Color.WHITE);
        this.requestFocus();

        person = new Girl(50,50,"icon/girl.png");
        person = new YellowDecorator("icon/yellow_skirt.png", person);
    }

    protected void paintComponent(Graphics g) {
        super.paintComponent(g);

        person.draw(g);
    }
}
```

Right click Test.java and then Run as -> Java Application again Result:

4. Change YellowDecorator **to** BlueDecorator **in** Canvas.java

```java
import java.awt.*;
import java.util.List;
import javax.swing.JPanel;
public class Canvas extends JPanel {
    Person person;

    public Canvas() {
        this.setLayout(null);
        this.setBackground(Color.WHITE);
        this.requestFocus();

        person = new Girl(50,50,"icon/girl.png");
        person = new BlueDecorator("icon/blue_skirt.png", person);
    }

    protected void paintComponent(Graphics g) {
        super.paintComponent(g);

        person.draw(g);
    }
}
```

Right click Test.java **and then** Run as -> Java Application again **Result:**

Prototype Pattern Shallow Clone

Prototype Pattern :
Specify the kinds of objects you create, and create new ones by copying them.

Analysis:
1. Objects have the ability to clone and need to implement the Cloneable interface

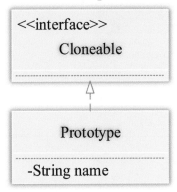

Shallow clones: only copy basic data types

Prototype.java in package com.clone.shallow;

```java
public class Prototype implements Cloneable {
    private String name;

    public Prototype(String name) {
        super();
        this.name = name;
    }

    public String getName() {
        return name;
    }

    protected Object clone() {
        Prototype p = null;
        try {
            p = (Prototype) super.clone();
        } catch (CloneNotSupportedException e) {
            e.printStackTrace();
        }
        return p;
    }
}
```

1. Create a Test class : TestClone.java in package com.clone.shallow;

```java
public class TestClone {

    public static void main(String[] args) {

        Prototype p = new Prototype("David");
        System.out.println(p.getName());

        System.out.println("--------------------");

        Prototype p2 = (Prototype) p.clone();
        System.out.println(p2.getName());
    }
}
```

Right click TestClone.java and then Run as -> Java Application Result:

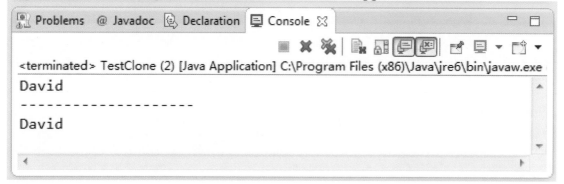

Prototype Pattern Deep Clone

Prototype Pattern :

Specify the kinds of objects you create, and create new ones by copying them.

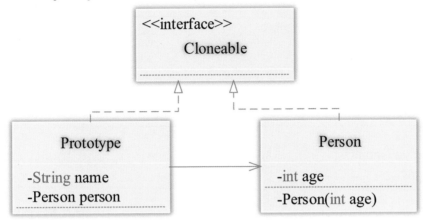

Deep clones: can copy object.

Person.java in package com.clone.deep;

```java
public class Person implements Cloneable {
    private int age;

    public Person(int age) {
        super();
        this.age = age;
    }

    public int getAge() {
        return age;
    }

    protected Object clone() {
        try {
            return super.clone();
        } catch (CloneNotSupportedException e) {
            e.printStackTrace();
        }
        return null;
    }
}
```

Prototype.java in package com.clone.deep;

```java
public class Prototype implements Cloneable {
    private String name;
    private Person person;

    public Prototype(String name) {
        super();
        this.name = name;
    }

    public String getName() {
        return name;
    }

    public void setName(String name) {
        this.name = name;
    }

    public Person getPerson() {
        return person;
    }

    public void setPerson(Person person) {
        this.person = person;
    }

    protected Object clone() {
        Prototype p = null;
        try {
            p = (Prototype) super.clone();

            if (person != null) {
                Object obj = person.clone();
                p.person = (Person) obj;
            }
        } catch (CloneNotSupportedException e) {
            e.printStackTrace();
        }
        return p;
    }
}
```

1. Create a Test class : TestDeepClone.java in package com.clone.deep;

```java
public class TestDeepClone {

    public static void main(String[] args) {

        Prototype p = new Prototype("David");
        p.setPerson(new Person(20));
        System.out.println(p.getName() + "," + p.getPerson().getAge());

        System.out.println("-------------------------");

        Prototype p2 = (Prototype) p.clone();
        System.out.println(p2.getName() + "," + p.getPerson().getAge());
    }
}
```

Right click TestDeepClone.java and then Run as -> Java Application Result:

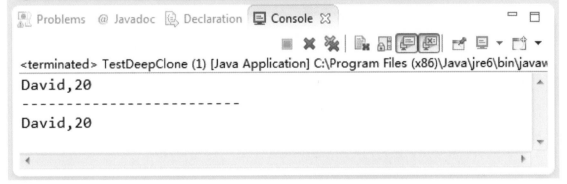

Prototype Pattern Case

1. Example :

Draw a rectangle on the canvas, click the mouse to select the rectangle, the rectangle border becomes red, then press Ctrl+C to copy and clone rectangle to the clipboard, finally press Ctrl+V to paste and create a new rectangle on the canvas

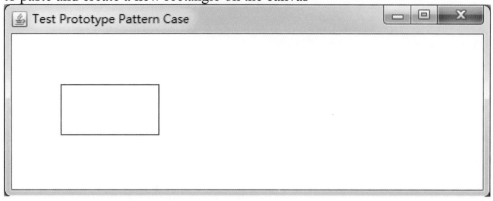

Mouse click rectangle

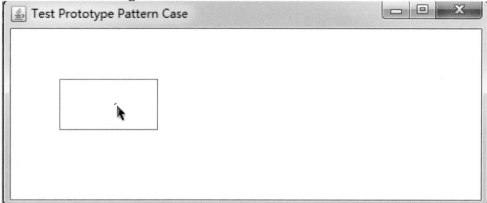

Press Ctrl+C to copy and clone rectangle to the clipboard, finally press Ctrl+V to paste and create a new rectangle on the canvas

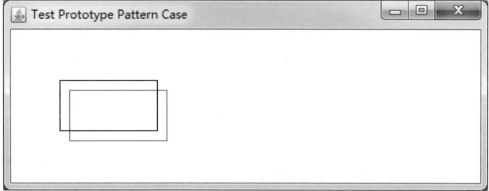

Analysis:

1. Create 1 class: Rectangle that implement the clone interface: Cloneable.

2. The rectangle has a attribute: selected, if it is not selected, draw a black rectangle, if it has been selected, draw a red rectangle.

```
public void draw(Graphics g){
   if(selected){
      g.setColor(Color.RED);
      g.drawRect(this.x, this.y, this.width, this.height);
      g.setColor(Color.BLACK);
   }else{
      g.drawRect(this.x, this.y, this.width, this.height);
   }
}
```

3. Create a method: boolean contains(int x, int y) that check if the mouse click is inside the rectangle.

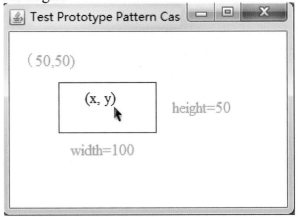

```
public boolean contains(int x, int y){
   if((x > this.x && x - this.x < width) && (y > this.y && y - this.y < height)){
      return true;
   }
   return false;
}
```

4. Create 1 class: Canvas . Each rectangle is added to LinkedList<Rectangle>, and then drawn on the canvas

```java
public Canvas() {
   rectList.addFirst(new Rectangle(50, 50, 100, 50));
}

protected void paintComponent(Graphics g) {
   super.paintComponent(g);

   for(int i=0;i<rectList.size();i++){
      Rectangle rectangle = rectList.get(i);
      rectangle.draw(g);
   }
}
```

5. Canvas implements the mouse listener interface: MouseListener. Set the selected rectangle's attribute selected= true, and add the rectangle to the head of LinkedList<Rectangle>. And then repaint canvas let the method paintComponent(Graphics g) will invoked automatically.

```java
public void mouseClicked(MouseEvent e) {

   boolean hasSelected = false;
   for(int i=0;i<rectList.size();i++){
      Rectangle rectangle = rectList.get(i);
      if(!hasSelected && rectangle.contains(e.getX(), e.getY())){
         rectangle.setSelected(true);
         rectList.remove(i);
         rectList.addFirst(rectangle);
         hasSelected = true;
      }else{
         rectangle.setSelected(false);
      }
   }
   repaint();
}
```

6. Canvas implements the key listener interface: KeyListener. press Ctrl+C to copy and clone rectangle to the clipboard, finally press Ctrl+V to paste and create a new rectangle on the canvas

```java
public void keyPressed(KeyEvent e) {
    int keyCode = e.getKeyCode();
    if(e.isControlDown() && keyCode == KeyEvent.VK_C){
        if(rectList.size()>0){
            Rectangle rentangle = rectList.getFirst();
            if(rentangle.isSelected()){
                clipBoard = rentangle.clone();
            }
        }
    }else if(e.isControlDown() && keyCode == KeyEvent.VK_V){
        if(clipBoard!=null){
            Rectangle rentangle = (Rectangle)clipBoard;
            rentangle.setX(rentangle.getX() + 10);
            rentangle.setY(rentangle.getY() + 10);
            rectList.getFirst().setSelected(false);
            rectList.addFirst(rentangle);
            clipBoard=null;
            repaint();
        }
    }
}
```

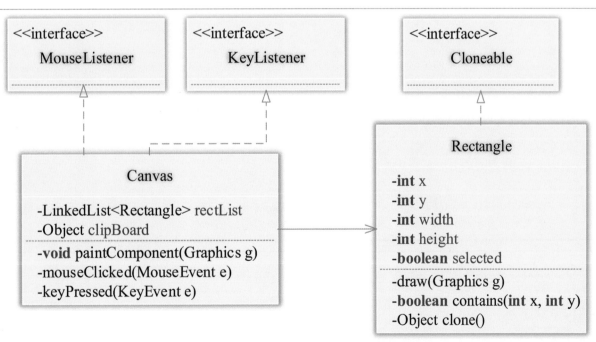

Create all classes in project test/com.prototype.cases

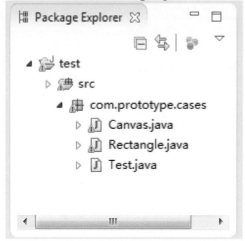

Rectangle.java **in package** com.prototype.cases;

```java
import java.awt.*;
import java.awt.image.BufferedImage;
public  class Rectangle  implements Cloneable{
   protected int x;
   protected int y;
   protected int width;
   protected int height;
   protected boolean selected = false;

   public Rectangle(int x, int y, int width, int height){
      this.x = x;
      this.y = y;
      this.width = width;
      this.height = height;
   }

   public void draw(Graphics g){
      if(selected){
         g.setColor(Color.RED);
         g.drawRect(this.x, this.y, this.width, this.height);
         g.setColor(Color.BLACK);
      }else{
         g.drawRect(this.x, this.y, this.width, this.height);
      }
   }
}
```

```java
public boolean contains(int x, int y){
    if((x > this.x && x - this.x < width) && (y > this.y && y - this.y < height)){
        return true;
    }
    return false;
}

public boolean isSelected() {
    return selected;
}

public void setSelected(boolean selected) {
    this.selected = selected;
}


public void setX(int x) {
    this.x = x;
}
public int getX(){
    return this.x;
}

public void setY(int y) {
    this.y = y;
}
public int getY(){
    return this.y;
}

protected Object clone() {
    try {
        return super.clone();
    } catch (CloneNotSupportedException e) {
        e.printStackTrace();
    }
    return null;
}
}
```

Canvas.java in package com.prototype.cases;

```java
import java.awt.*;
import java.awt.event.*;
import java.util.*;
import javax.swing.*;
public class Canvas extends JPanel implements MouseListener, KeyListener {
    private LinkedList<Rectangle> rectList = new LinkedList<Rectangle>();
    private Object clipBoard;

    public Canvas() {
        this.setLayout(null);
        this.setBackground(Color.WHITE);
        this.requestFocus();
        this.addMouseListener(this);
        this.addKeyListener(this);
        rectList.addFirst(new Rectangle(50, 50, 100, 50));
    }

    protected void paintComponent(Graphics g) {
        super.paintComponent(g);

        for(int i=0;i<rectList.size();i++){
            Rectangle rectangle = rectList.get(i);
            rectangle.draw(g);
        }
    }

    public void mouseClicked(MouseEvent e) {

        boolean hasSelected = false;
        for(int i=0;i<rectList.size();i++){
            Rectangle rectangle = rectList.get(i);
            if(!hasSelected && rectangle.contains(e.getX(), e.getY())){
                rectangle.setSelected(true);
                rectList.remove(i);
                rectList.addFirst(rectangle);
                hasSelected = true;
            }else{
                rectangle.setSelected(false);
            }
        }
        repaint();
    }
```

```java
public void mousePressed(MouseEvent e) {
}

public void mouseReleased(MouseEvent e) {
}

public void mouseEntered(MouseEvent e) {
}

public void mouseExited(MouseEvent e) {
}

public void keyPressed(KeyEvent e) {
   int keyCode = e.getKeyCode();
   if(e.isControlDown() && keyCode == KeyEvent.VK_C){
     if(rectList.size()>0){
        Rectangle rentangle = rectList.getFirst();
        if(rentangle.isSelected()){
           clipBoard = rentangle.clone();
        }
     }
   }else  if(e.isControlDown() && keyCode == KeyEvent.VK_V){
       if(clipBoard!=null){
          Rectangle rentangle = (Rectangle)clipBoard;
          rentangle.setX(rentangle.getX() + 10);
          rentangle.setY(rentangle.getY() + 10);
          rectList.getFirst().setSelected(false);
          rectList.addFirst(rentangle);
          clipBoard=null;
          repaint();
       }
   }
}

public void keyReleased(KeyEvent e) {
}

public void keyTyped(KeyEvent e) {
}
}
```

1. Create a Test class : Test.java in package com.prototype.cases;

```java
import java.awt.*;
import javax.swing.*;

public class Test {
    private static Canvas canvas;

    public static void main(String[] args) {
        JFrame frame = new JFrame("Test Prototype Pattern Case");
        canvas = new Canvas();
        frame.add(canvas, BorderLayout.CENTER);
        frame.setSize(500, 300);
        frame.setVisible(true);
        frame.setDefaultCloseOperation(JFrame.EXIT_ON_CLOSE);
        frame.setFocusable(false);
        canvas.requestFocus();
    }
}
```

Right click Test.java and then Run as -> Java Application Result:

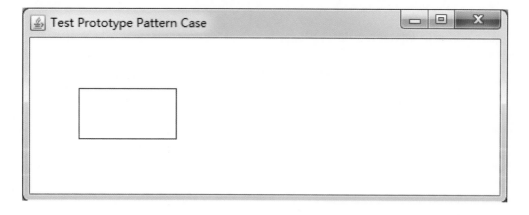

Mouse click rectangle

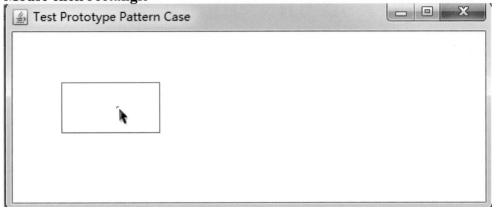

Press Ctrl+C to copy and clone rectangle to the clipboard, finally press Ctrl+V to paste and create a new rectangle on the canvas

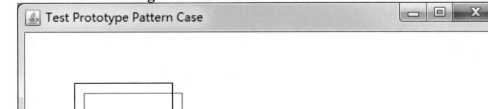

Bridge Pattern Principle

Bridge Pattern : Separates an object's interface from its implementation. Decouple an abstraction from its implementation so that can vary independently.

1. Example: Different people can wear different clothes

Analysis:
1. Create 1 abstract class: Clothing.
2. Clothing have 2 implementation classes: Jacket, Trouser.
3. Create 1 abstract class: Person. and then create abstract method: dress() that let different people can wear different clothes
4. Person have 2 implementation classes: Man, Lady.

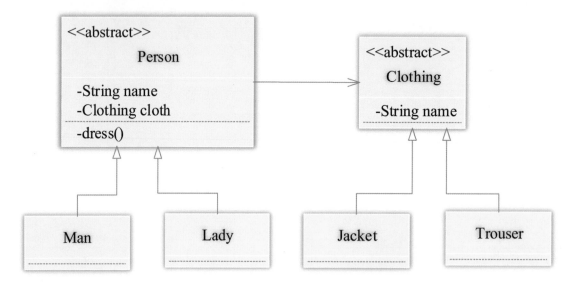

Clothing.java in package com.bridge.principle;

```java
public abstract class Clothing {

    protected String name;

    public Clothing(String name) {
        this.name = name;
    }

    public String getName() {
        return name;
    }
}
```

Jacket.java in package com.bridge.principle;

```java
public class Jacket extends Clothing {

    public Jacket(String name) {
        super(name);
    }
}
```

Trouser.java in package com.bridge.principle;

```java
public class Trouser extends Clothing {

    public Trouser(String name) {
        super(name);
    }
}
```

Person.java in package com.bridge.principle;

```java
public abstract class Person {
    protected String name;
    protected Clothing cloth;

    public Person(String name) {
        super();
        this.name = name;
    }

    public String getName() {
        return name;
    }

    public Clothing getCloth() {
        return cloth;
    }

    public void setCloth(Clothing cloth) {
        this.cloth = cloth;
    }

    public abstract void dress();
}
```

Man.java in package com.bridge.principle;

```java
public class Man extends Person {

    public Man(String name) {
        super(name);
    }

    @Override
    public void dress() {
        System.out.println(name + " wear " + cloth.getName());
    }
}
```

Lady.java in package com.bridge.principle;

```java
public class Lady extends Person {
    public Lady(String name) {
        super(name);
    }

    public void dress() {
        System.out.println(name + " wear " + cloth.getName());
    }
}
```

2. Create a Test class : TestBridge.java in package com.bridge.principle;

```java
public class TestBridge {
    public static void main(String[] args) {
        Person man = new Man("Man");
        Person lady = new Lady("Lady");

        Clothing jacket = new Jacket("Jacket");
        Clothing trouser = new Trouser("Trouser");

        man.setCloth(jacket); //Man wear Jacket
        man.dress();

        man.setCloth(trouser); //Man wear Trouser
        man.dress();

        lady.setCloth(jacket); //Lady wear Jacket
        lady.dress();

        lady.setCloth(trouser); //Lady wear Trouser
        lady.dress();
    }
}
```

Right click TestBridge.java and then Run as -> Java Application Result:

```
Problems  @ Javadoc  Declaration  Console
Man wear Jacket
Man wear Trouser
Lady wear Jacket
Lady wear Trouser
```

Bridge Pattern Case

1. Example: Different airplane fire different bullets

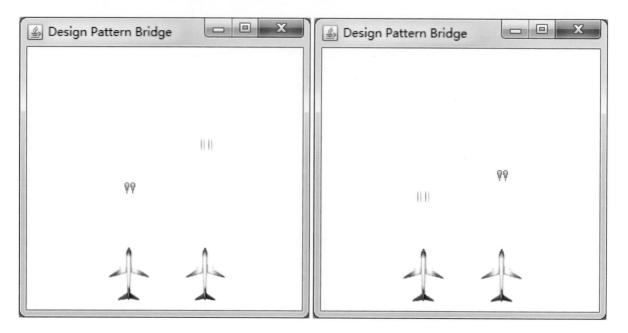

Analysis:

1. All planes and bullets are called sprite, because they have some of the same attributes and behaviors, we can create a abstract class: Sprite.

Sprite have attributes: x, y, width, height of image and visible in the canvas?

Sprite have methods: draw(Graphics g) can draw image on canvas.

                 move(int distanceX, int distanceY) can move image on canvas.

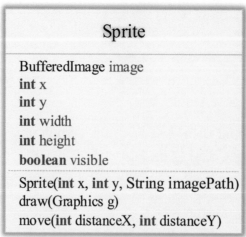

2. Create 2 classes: Plane, Bullet inherit from Sprite.
   and then create 2 classes: BlueBullet, RedBullet inherit from Bullet
   and then create 2 classes: BluePlane, RedPlane inherit from Plane
   BluePlane can load and fire BlueBullet.
   RedPlane can load and fire RedBullet.
   BluePlane can load and fire RedBullet.
   RedPlane can load and fire BlueBullet.

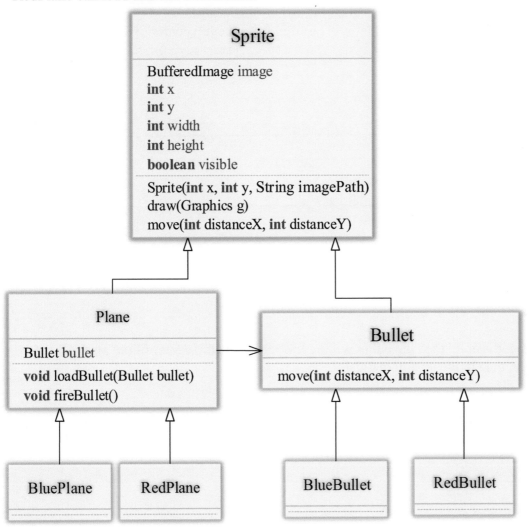

3. Plane can load bullet, we can create a method: loadBullet(Bullet bullet)

```java
public void loadBullet(Bullet bullet){
    this.bullet = bullet;
}
```

Plane can fire bullet, we can create a method in Plane: fireBullet()
If the bullet is not visible, then the bullet will be fired from the top center of the plane.

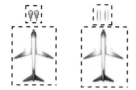

```java
public void fireBullet(){
    if(!bullet.isVisible()){
        int x = this.x+this.width/2-bullet.getWidth()/2;
        int y = this.y- bullet.getHeight();
        bullet.setX(x);
        bullet.setY(y);
        bullet.setVisible(true);
    }
}
```

If the bullet is not visible, then the bullet will be fired from the top center of the plane. If the bullet is visible, then move up automatically.

```java
private void bulletMove(){
    if( bluePlane.getBullet().isVisible()){
        bluePlane.getBullet().move(0, -3);
    }else{
        bluePlane.fireBullet();
    }

    if( redPlane.getBullet().isVisible()){
        redPlane.getBullet().move(0, -3);
    }else{
        redPlane.fireBullet();
    }
}
```

If the bullet moves out of the top of the canvas, set visible=false, and the bullet will re-launch. We can override the Sprite method: move(int distanceX, int distanceY)

```java
public void move(int distanceX, int distanceY){
    this.x = this.x + distanceX;
    this.y = this.y + distanceY;
    if(this.y + this.height <=0){
        this.setVisible(false);
    }
}
```

4. Create BluePlane to load BlueBullet and RedPlane to load RedBullet on Canvas:

```java
public Canvas() {
    this.setLayout(null);
    this.setBackground(Color.WHITE);

    redPlane = new RedPlane(80, 200, "images/red_plane.png");
    redPlane.loadBullet(new RedBullet(-100, -100,"images/red_bullet.png"));

    bluePlane = new BluePlane(160, 200,"images/blue_plane.png");
    bluePlane.loadBullet(new BlueBullet(-100, -100,"images/blue_bullet.png"));
}
```

5. Draw BluePlane, BlueBullet, RedPlane, RedBullet on Canvas:

```java
protected void paintComponent(Graphics g) {
    super.paintComponent(g);

    bluePlane.draw(g);
    bluePlane.getBullet().draw(g);

    redPlane.draw(g);
    redPlane.getBullet().draw(g);

    bulletMove();
}
```

6. Press the up, down, left, right key to move BluePlane.
   Press the E, D, S, F key to move RedPlane.

```java
public void keyPressed(KeyEvent e) {
    int keyCode = e.getKeyCode();
    if(keyCode == KeyEvent.VK_E){
        redPlane.move(0, -3);
    }else if(keyCode == KeyEvent.VK_D){
        redPlane.move(0, 3);
    }else if(keyCode == KeyEvent.VK_F){
        redPlane.move(3, 0);
    }else if(keyCode ==  KeyEvent.VK_S){
        redPlane.move(-3, 0);
    }

    if(keyCode == KeyEvent.VK_UP){
        bluePlane.move(0, -3);
    }else if(keyCode == KeyEvent.VK_DOWN){
        bluePlane.move(0, 3);
    }else if(keyCode == KeyEvent.VK_RIGHT){
        bluePlane.move(3, 0);
    }else if(keyCode ==  KeyEvent.VK_LEFT){
        bluePlane.move(-3, 0);
    }
    Canvas.this.repaint();
}
```

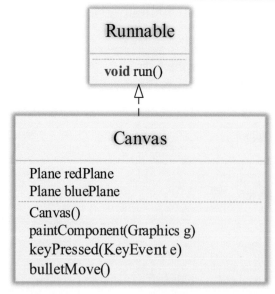

Create all classes in project test/com.bridge.cases

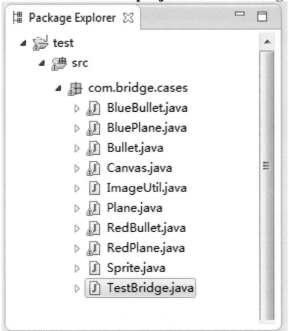

Copy ImageUtil.java **code here from the previous chapter:** Animation

Sprite.java **in package** com.bridge.cases;

```java
import java.awt.Graphics;
import java.awt.image.BufferedImage;

abstract class Sprite {
    protected int x; // x coordinate of Canvas
    protected int y; // y coordinate of Canvas
    protected int width;
    protected int height;
    protected BufferedImage image;
    protected boolean visible;

    public Sprite(int x, int y, String imagePath){
        this.x = x;
        this.y = y;
        this.image=ImageUtil.loadImage(imagePath);
        this.width = this.image.getWidth();
        this.height = this.image.getHeight();
    }
}
```

```java
    public void draw(Graphics g){
       g.drawImage(image, this.x, this.y, null);
    }

    public void move(int distanceX, int distanceY){
       this.x = this.x + distanceX;
       this.y = this.y + distanceY;
    }

    public int getWidth() {
       return width;
    }

    public int getHeight() {
       return height;
    }

    public int getX() {
       return x;
    }

    public void setX(int x) {
       this.x = x;
    }

    public int getY() {
       return y;
    }

    public void setY(int y) {
       this.y = y;
    }

    public boolean isVisible() {
       return visible;
    }

    public void setVisible(boolean visible) {
       this.visible = visible;
    }
}
```

Bullet.java in package com.bridge.cases;

```java
import java.awt.image.BufferedImage;

public class Bullet  extends Sprite{

    public Bullet(int x, int y, String imagePath) {
        super(x, y, imagePath);
    }

    public void move(int distanceX, int distanceY){
        this.x = this.x + distanceX;
        this.y = this.y + distanceY;
        if(this.y + this.height <=0){
            this.setVisible(false);
        }
    }
}
```

BlueBullet.java in package com.bridge.cases;

```java
import java.awt.image.BufferedImage;

public class BlueBullet  extends Bullet{

    public BlueBullet(int x, int y, String imagePath) {
        super(x, y, imagePath);
    }
}
```

RedBullet.java in package com.bridge.cases;

```java
import java.awt.image.BufferedImage;

public class RedBullet  extends Bullet{

    public RedBullet(int x, int y, String imagePath) {
        super(x, y, imagePath);
    }
}
```

Plane.java in package com.bridge.cases;

```java
import java.awt.image.BufferedImage;

public class Plane  extends Sprite{
    protected Bullet bullet;

    public Plane(int x, int y, String imagePath) {
        super(x, y, imagePath);
    }

    public void loadBullet(Bullet bullet){
        this.bullet = bullet;
    }

    public void fireBullet(){
        if(!bullet.isVisible()){
            int x = this.x+this.width/2-bullet.getWidth()/2;
            int y = this.y- bullet.getHeight();
            bullet.setX(x);
            bullet.setY(y);
            bullet.setVisible(true);
        }
    }

    public Bullet getBullet(){
        return this.bullet;
    }
}
```

BluePlane.java in package com.bridge.cases;

```java
import java.awt.image.BufferedImage;

public class BluePlane  extends Plane{

    public BluePlane(int x, int y, String imagePath) {
        super(x, y, imagePath);
    }
}
```

RedPlane.java in package com.bridge.cases;

```java
import java.awt.image.BufferedImage;
public class RedPlane  extends Plane{

  public RedPlane(int x, int y, String imagePath) {
    super(x, y, imagePath);
  }
}
```

Canvas.java in package com.bridge.cases;

```java
import java.awt.*;
import java.awt.event.*;
import javax.swing.*;
public class Canvas extends JPanel  implements Runnable{
  private boolean isRun = true;
  private Plane bluePlane;
  private Plane redPlane;

  public Canvas() {
    this.setLayout(null);
    this.setBackground(Color.WHITE);

    redPlane = new RedPlane(80, 200, "images/red_plane.png");
    redPlane.loadBullet(new RedBullet(-100, -100,"images/red_bullet.png"));

    bluePlane = new BluePlane(160, 200,"images/blue_plane.png");
    bluePlane.loadBullet(new BlueBullet(-100, -100,"images/blue_bullet.png"));

    new Thread(this).start();
    this.addKeyListener(keyListener);
  }

  protected void paintComponent(Graphics g) {
    super.paintComponent(g);
    bluePlane.draw(g);
    bluePlane.getBullet().draw(g);
    redPlane.draw(g);
    redPlane.getBullet().draw(g);

    bulletMove();
  }
```

```java
private KeyAdapter keyListener = new KeyAdapter(){
   public void keyPressed(KeyEvent e) {
      int keyCode = e.getKeyCode();
      if(keyCode == KeyEvent.VK_E){
         redPlane.move(0, -3);
      }else if(keyCode == KeyEvent.VK_D){
         redPlane.move(0, 3);
      }else if(keyCode == KeyEvent.VK_F){
         redPlane.move(3, 0);
      }else if(keyCode ==  KeyEvent.VK_S){
         redPlane.move(-3, 0);
      }

      if(keyCode == KeyEvent.VK_UP){
         bluePlane.move(0, -3);
      }else if(keyCode == KeyEvent.VK_DOWN){
         bluePlane.move(0, 3);
      }else if(keyCode == KeyEvent.VK_RIGHT){
         bluePlane.move(3, 0);
      }else if(keyCode ==  KeyEvent.VK_LEFT){
         bluePlane.move(-3, 0);
      }
      Canvas.this.repaint();
   }
};

private void bulletMove(){
   if( bluePlane.getBullet().isVisible()){
      bluePlane.getBullet().move(0, -3);
   }else{
      bluePlane.fireBullet();
   }

   if( redPlane.getBullet().isVisible()){
      redPlane.getBullet().move(0, -3);
   }else{
      redPlane.fireBullet();
   }
}
```

```
    public void run() {
       while(isRun){
          try {
             Thread.sleep(200);
             Canvas.this.repaint();
          } catch (InterruptedException e) {
             e.printStackTrace();
          }
       }
    }
 }
```

2. Create a Test class : TestBridge.java in package com.bridge.cases;

```
import java.awt.BorderLayout;
import javax.swing.JFrame;
public class TestBridge {
    public static void main(String[] args) {
       JFrame frame = new JFrame("Design Pattern Bridge");
       Canvas canvas = new Canvas();
       frame.add(canvas, BorderLayout.CENTER);
       frame.setSize(300, 300);
       canvas.setFocusable(true);
       frame.setVisible(true);
       canvas.requestFocus();
    }
}
```

Right click TestBridge.java and then Run as -> Java Application Result:

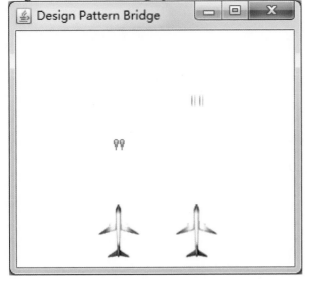

Change code in Canvas BluePlane to load RedBullet and RedPlane to load BlueBullet

```
public Canvas() {
    this.setLayout(null);
    this.setBackground(Color.WHITE);

    redPlane = new RedPlane(80, 200, "images/red_plane.png");
    redPlane.loadBullet(new BlueBullet(-100, -100,"images/blue_bullet.png"));

    bluePlane = new BluePlane(160, 200,"images/blue_plane.png");
    bluePlane.loadBullet(new RedBullet(-100, -100,"images/red_bullet.png"));

    new Thread(this).start();
    this.addKeyListener(keyListener);
}
```

Right click TestBridge.java and then Run as -> Java Application again Result:

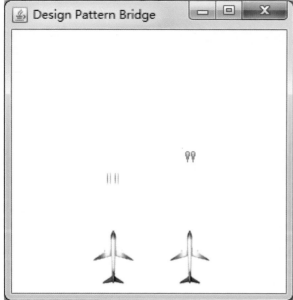

FlyWeight Pattern Principle

FlyWeight Pattern : A flyweight is a shared object, A fine-grained instance used for efficient sharing. Use sharing to support large numbers of fine-grained objects efficiently.

1. Example: Some data can be stored in the cache. The client can get the data directly from the cache to improve the access speed.

Analysis:
1. Create a class: Cache that can store and get various objects.
   Create a method: put(String key, Object value) to store various objects.
   Create a method: Object get(String key) to get object by key.

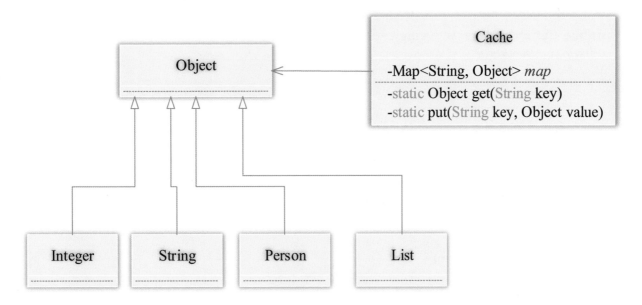

Cache.java in package com.flyweight.principle;

```java
import java.util.*;
public class Cache {
    private static Map<String, Object> map = new HashMap<String, Object>();

    public static Object get(String key) {
        return map.get(key);
    }

    public static void put(String key, Object value) {
        map.put(key, value);
    }

    public static void remove(String key) {
        map.remove(key);
    }
}
```

Person.java in package com.flyweight.principle;

```java
public class Person {
    private String name;

    public Person(String name) {
        this.name = name;
    }

    public String getName() {
        return name;
    }
}
```

2. Create a Test class : TestCache.java in package com.flyweight.principle;

```java
import java.util.*;

public class TestCache {

    public static void main(String[] args) {
        //Basic data types are stored in the cache
        Cache.put("1", 1000);

        //String are stored in the cache
        Cache.put("name", "Grace");

        //Object are stored in the cache
        Cache.put("person", new Person("Sala"));

        //Get data from the cache
        System.out.println(Cache.get("1"));
        System.out.println(Cache.get("name"));
        Person p = (Person) Cache.get("person");
        System.out.println(p.getName());
    }
}
```

Right click TestCache.java and then Run as -> Java Application Result:

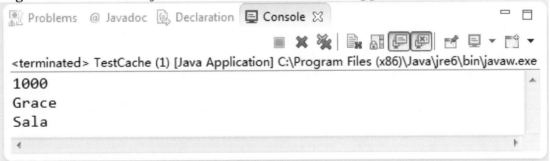

FlyWeight Pattern Case

1. Example: Internationalization is a mechanism to create such an application that can be adapted to different languages and regions. First load the xml data into the cache and then fetch the data from the cache

Analysis:

1. Create 2 Internationalization xml:
   English xml: message_en_US.xml.

```
<?xml version="1.0" encoding="UTF-8"?>
<resources>
  <item key="name">Name</item>
  <item key="gender">Male</item>
</resources>
```

   Chinese xml: message_zh_CN.xml.

```
<?xml version="1.0" encoding="UTF-8"?>
<resources>
  <item key="name">姓名</item>
  <item key="gender">男</item>
</resources>
```

2. Create 1 class: Messages to read message_en_US.xml, message_zh_CN.xml

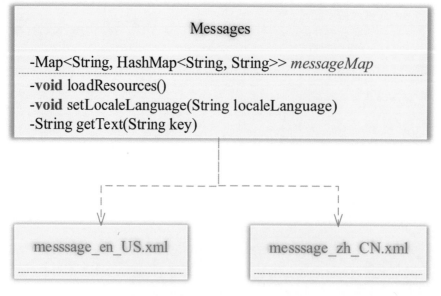

Each language code corresponds to an xml file data store to HashMap
Example: en_US -> message_en_US.xml
        zh_CN -> message_zh_CN.xml
Each xml file data store as key -> value to HashMap
All data cache in HashMap, In the future, we can read data directly from the cache instead of repeatedly reading the xml file: String getText(String key)

```java
private static Map<String, HashMap<String, String>> messageMap = new
HashMap<String, HashMap<String, String>>();

public static String getText(String key) {
    Map<String, String> bundleMap = messageMap.get(localeLanguage);
    return bundleMap.get(key);
}
```

Create 2 xml: message_en_US.xml, message_zh_CN.xml **file to test/src**

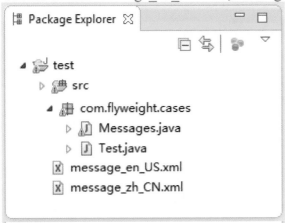

About How to read xml file, please refer to the previous chapter Factory Pattern Case

Messages.java in package com.flyweight.cases;

```java
import java.io.*;
import java.util.*;
import org.dom4j.*;
import org.dom4j.io.SAXReader;
public class Messages {
    private static Map<String, HashMap<String, String>> messageMap = new
HashMap<String, HashMap<String, String>>();
    private static String[] locales = { "en_US", "zh_CN" };
    private static String localeLanguage = "en_US";
```

```java
    public static String getText(String key) {
       Map<String, String> bundleMap = messageMap.get(localeLanguage);
       return bundleMap.get(key);
    }

    public static void setLocaleLanguage(String localeLanguage) {
       Messages.localeLanguage = localeLanguage;
    }

    public static void loadResources() {
       messageMap.clear();
       for (String locale : locales) {
          SAXReader reader = new SAXReader();
          Object objRef = new Object();
          String absolutePath = objRef.getClass().getResource("/").getPath() + "/message_" +
locale + ".xml";
          InputStream is = null;
          HashMap<String, String> bundleMap = new HashMap<String, String>();
          try {
             is = new FileInputStream(absolutePath);
             Document doc = reader.read(is); // convert xml to Document
             List<Element> elementList = doc.selectNodes("/resources/item");
             for (Element element : elementList) {
                String key = element.attributeValue("key");
                String value = element.getText();
                bundleMap.put(key, value);
                messageMap.put(locale, bundleMap);
             }
          } catch (Exception e) {
             e.printStackTrace();
          } finally {
             try {
                is.close();
             } catch (IOException e) {
                e.printStackTrace();
             }
          }
       }
    }
}
```

2. Create a Test class : Test.java in package com.flyweight.principle;

```java
public class Test {

    public static void main(String[] args) {
        Messages.loadResources();

        Messages.setLocaleLanguage("en_US");
        System.out.println("name = " + Messages.getText("name"));
        System.out.println("gender = " + Messages.getText("gender"));

        System.out.println("--------------------------------------");

        Messages.setLocaleLanguage("zh_CN");
        System.out.println("name = " + Messages.getText("name"));
        System.out.println("gender = " + Messages.getText("gender"));
    }
}
```

Right click Test.java and then Run as -> Java Application Result:

```
Console ☒                    ■ ✖ ✖ | ▤ ▤ ▣ ▣ | ☞ ▣ ▼ ☞ ▼ ☐ ▤
<terminated> Test (47) [Java Application] C:\Program Files (x86)\Java\jre6\bin\javaw.exe (202:
name = Name
gender = Male
------------------------------------------
name = 姓名
gender = 男
```

Chain Pattern Principle

Chain Pattern : A way of passing a request between a chain of objects. giving more than one object a chance to handle the request and pass the request along the chain until an object handles it.

1. Example: The resignation rrocess: what to do when employees leave.

In this chapter, we will discuss ways to develop a consistent employee exit procedure so employees, managers, HR representatives, and finacial know what needs to be done for verification.

Resignation Apply -> Financial Review -> Manager Review -> Approval

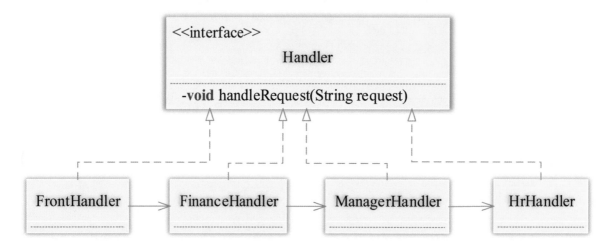

Handler.java in package com.chain.principle;

```
public interface Handler {

    public void handleRequest(String request);

}
```

FrontHandler.java in package com.chain.principle;

```java
public class FrontHandler implements Handler {
    private Handler nextHandler;

    public FrontHandler(Handler nextHandler) {
        this.nextHandler = nextHandler;
    }

    @Override
    public void handleRequest(String request) {
        if ("ResignationApply".equals(request)) {
            System.out.println("Resignation Apply");
            if (nextHandler != null)
                nextHandler.handleRequest("FinancialReview");
        }
    }
}
```

FinanceHandler.java in package com.chain.principle;

```java
public class FinanceHandler implements Handler {
    private Handler nextHandler;

    public FinanceHandler(Handler nextHandler) {
        this.nextHandler = nextHandler;
    }

    @Override
    public void handleRequest(String request) {
        if ("FinancialReview".equals(request)) {
            System.out.println("Financial Review Completed");
            if (nextHandler != null)
                nextHandler.handleRequest("ManagerReview");
        }
    }
}
```

ManagerHandler.java in package com.chain.principle;

```java
public class ManagerHandler implements Handler {
  private Handler nextHandler;

  public ManagerHandler(Handler nextHandler) {
    this.nextHandler = nextHandler;
  }

  @Override
  public void handleRequest(String request) {
    if ("ManagerReview".equals(request)) {
      System.out.println("Manager Review Completed");
      if (nextHandler != null)
        nextHandler.handleRequest("Approval");
    }
  }
}
```

HrHandler.java in package com.chain.principle;

```java
public class HrHandler implements Handler {
  private Handler nextHandler;

  public HrHandler (Handler nextHandler) {
    this.nextHandler = nextHandler;
  }

  @Override
  public void handleRequest(String request) {
    if ("Approval".equals(request)) {
      System.out.println("HR Approval");
      if (nextHandler != null)
        nextHandler.handleRequest("Approval Completed");
    }
  }
}
```

2. Create a Test class : TestHandler.java in package com.chain.principle;

```java
public class TestHandler {

    public static void main(String[] args) {

        Handler hrHandler = new HrHandler(null);
        Handler managerHandler = new ManagerHandler(hrHandler);
        Handler financeHandler = new FinanceHandler(managerHandler);
        Handler frontHandler = new FrontHandler(financeHandler);

        frontHandler.handleRequest("ResignationApply");
    }
}
```

Right click TestHandler.java and then Run as -> Java Application Result:

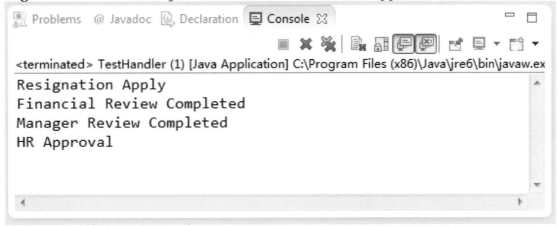

Chain Pattern Case

1. Java Web Filter or VereMVC Web Framework Interceptor is Chain Pattern.

http://en.verejava.com/?section_id=1697715673191

2. Example: Interceptor is an object that is invoked at the preprocessing and postprocessing of a request. In VereMVC, interceptor is used to perform operations such as:
Validation -> Authority Authentication -> Set Character -> Business Preprocessing etc.

Authority Authentication -> Set Character -> Business Preprocessing

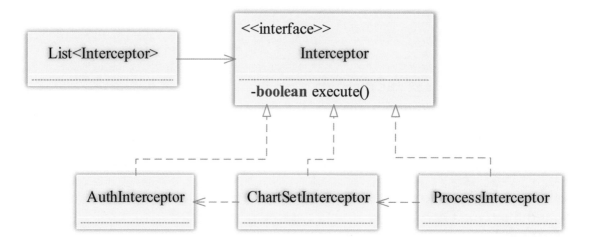

Interceptor.java in package com.chain.cases;

```java
public interface Interceptor {

    public boolean execute();

}
```

AuthInterceptor.java **in package com.chain.cases;**

```java
public class AuthInterceptor implements Interceptor {

    @Override
    public boolean execute() {
        System.out.println("Authority Authentication");
        return true;
    }
}
```

ChartSetInterceptor.java **in package com.chain.cases;**

```java
public class ChartSetInterceptor implements Interceptor {

    @Override
    public boolean execute() {
        System.out.println("Set Character");
        return true;
    }
}
```

ProcessInterceptor.java **in package com.chain.cases;**

```java
public class ProcessInterceptor implements Interceptor {

    @Override
    public boolean execute() {
        System.out.println("Business Preprocessing");
        return true;
    }
}
```

3. Create a Test class : TestIntercepter.java in package com.chain.cases;

```java
import java.util.*;

public class TestIntercepter {

  public static void main(String[] args) {

    List<Interceptor> interceptorList = new ArrayList<Interceptor>();
    interceptorList.add(new AuthInterceptor());
    interceptorList.add(new ChartSetInterceptor());
    interceptorList.add(new ProcessInterceptor());

    for (int i = 0; i < interceptorList.size(); i++) {
      Interceptor interceptor = interceptorList.get(i);
      boolean isNextInvoke = interceptor.execute();

      if (!isNextInvoke) {
        break;
      }
    }
  }
}
```

Right click TestIntercepter.java and then Run as -> Java Application Result:

```
Problems  @ Javadoc  Declaration  Console

<terminated> TestIntercepter (1) [Java Application] C:\Program Files (x86)\Java\jre6\bin\javaw
Authority Authentication
Set Character
Business Preprocessing
```

Iterator Pattern Principle

Iterator Pattern : Provide a way to access the elements of an aggregate object sequentially without exposing its underlying representation.

1. Implement the iterator in Java

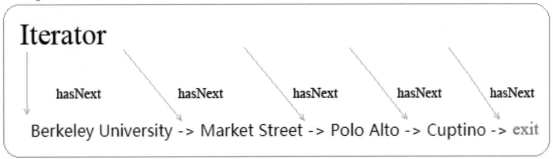

Analysis:

1. Create an interface: List and the implementation class: ArrayList. Create 4 methods:
   add(Object element): is used for adding an element to the ArrayList
   Object get(int index): is used for fetching an element from the list
   int size():is used to get the number of elements in this list
   Iterator iterator(): is used to iterate elements one-by-one from a List
2. Create an interface: Iterator and the implementation class: IteratorImpl.
   boolean hasNext(): Returns true if the iteration has more elements.
   Object next():It returns the next element in List

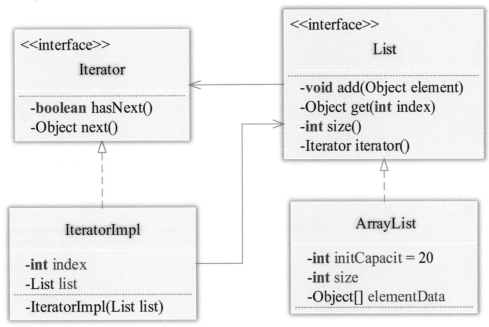

Iterator.java in package com.iterator.principle;

```java
public interface Iterator {

    public boolean hasNext();
    public Object next();
}
```

IteratorImpl.java in package com.iterator.principle;

```java
public class IteratorImpl implements Iterator {
    private int index;
    private List list;

    public IteratorImpl(List list) {
        this.list = list;
    }

    public boolean hasNext() {
        return index < list.size();
    }

    public Object next() {
        Object element = null;
        if (index < list.size()) {
            element = list.get(index);
            index++;
        }
        return element;
    }
}
```

List.java in package com.iterator.principle;

```java
public interface List {

    public void add(Object element);
    public Object get(int index);
    public int size();
    public Iterator iterator();
}
```

ArrayList.java in package com.iterator.principle;

```java
import java.util.Arrays;

public class ArrayList implements List {
    private int initCapacit = 20;
    private int size;
    private Object[] elementData;

    public ArrayList() {
        elementData = new Object[initCapacit];
    }

    public void add(Object element) {
        if (size < initCapacit) {
            elementData[size] = element;
            size++;
        } else {
            elementData = Arrays.copyOf(elementData, size);
            elementData[size] = element;
            size++;
        }
    }

    public Object get(int index) {
        return elementData[index];
    }

    public int size() {
        return size;
    }

    public Iterator iterator() {
        return new IteratorImpl(this);
    }
}
```

3. Create a Test class : TestIterator.java in package com.iterator.principle;

```java
public class TestIterator {

  public static void main(String[] args) {
    List list = new ArrayList();
    list.add("Berkeley University");
    list.add("Market Street");
    list.add("Polo Alto");
    list.add("Cuptino");

    Iterator iter = list.iterator();
    while (iter.hasNext()) {
      Object obj = iter.next();
      System.out.println(obj);
    }
  }
}
```

Right click TestIterator.java and then Run as -> Java Application Result:

```
Problems  @ Javadoc  Declaration  Console ⌗

<terminated> TestIterator (3) [Java Application] C:\Program Files (x86)\Java\jre6\bin\javaw.ex
Berkeley University
Market Street
Polo Alto
Cuptino
```

Mediator Pattern Principle

Mediator Pattern : Mediator promotes loose coupling by keeping objects from referring to each other explicitly, and it lets you vary their interaction independently.

1. Example: Servers communicate with each other, and each server needs to interact with other servers, this is an over-coupled system.

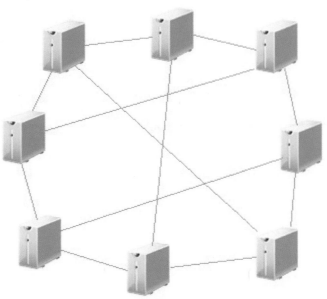

We add a Switch as a mediator. In this star structure, the Server no longer interacts with another Server through direct contact; it interacts through the Switch. Switch ensures the stability of the object structure, and if add new server will not cause a lot of modification.

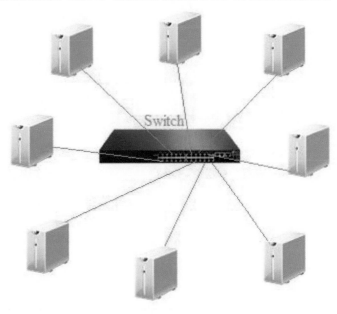

Analysis:

1. Create an abstract class: Server that define the interface from Server to the mediator object

2. Create 2 implementation class: ServerA, ServerB and then create 2 methods: sendMessage(String message) and receiveMessage(String message). ServerA send a message and calls the changed(Server server) method of SwitchMediator to notify ServerB. ServerB receives the message

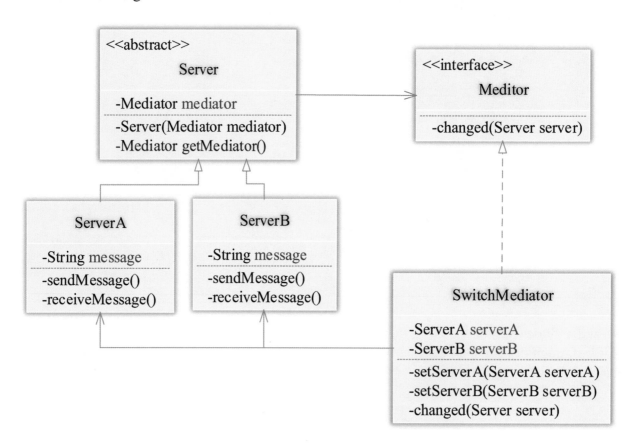

Server.java in package com.mediator.principle;

```java
public abstract class Server {
  private Mediator mediator;

  public Server(Mediator mediator){
    this.mediator = mediator;
  }

  public Mediator getMediator() {
    return mediator;
  }
}
```

ServerA.java in package com.mediator.principle;

```java
public class ServerA extends Server {
  private String message;

  public ServerA(Mediator mediator) {
    super(mediator);
  }

  public void sendMessage(String message){
    this.message = message;
    getMediator().changed(this);
  }

  public void receiveMessage(String message){
    if("ServerB_Port_201".equals(message)){
      System.out.println("ServerA receive message: "+message);
      System.out.println("ServerA disconnect with "+ message);
    }else if("ServerB_Port_200".equals(message)){
      System.out.println("ServerA receive message: "+message);
      System.out.println("ServerA connect with "+message+" successfully");
    }
  }

  public String getMessage() {
    return message;
  }
}
```

ServerB.java in package com.mediator.principle;

```java
public class ServerB extends Server {
   private String message;

   public ServerB(Mediator mediator) {
      super(mediator);
   }

   public void sendMessage(String message){
      this.message = message;
      getMediator().changed(this);
   }

   public void receiveMessage(String message){
      if("ServerA_Port_201".equals(message)){
         System.out.println("ServerB receive message: "+message);
         System.out.println("ServerB disconnect with "+message);
      }else if("ServerA_Port_200".equals(message)){
         System.out.println("ServerB receive message: "+message);
         System.out.println("ServerB connect with "+message+" successfully");
      }
   }

   public String getMessage() {
      return message;
   }
}
```

Mediator.java in package com.mediator.principle;

```java
public interface Mediator {

  public void changed(Server server);
}
```

SwitchMediator.java in package com.mediator.principle;

```java
public class SwitchMediator implements Mediator{
  private ServerA serverA;
  private ServerB serverB;

  public void setServerA(ServerA serverA) {
    this.serverA = serverA;
  }

  public void setServerB(ServerB serverB) {
    this.serverB = serverB;
  }

  @Override
  public void changed(Server server) {
    if(server instanceof ServerA){
      ServerA serverA = (ServerA)server;
      serverB.receiveMessage(serverA.getMessage());
    }else if(server instanceof ServerB){
      ServerB serverB = (ServerB)server;
      serverA.receiveMessage(serverB.getMessage());
    }
  }
}
```

2. Create a Test class : Test.java in package com.mediator.principle;

```java
public class Test {

    public static void main(String[] args) {
        SwitchMediator mediator = new SwitchMediator();

        ServerA serverA = new ServerA(mediator);
        ServerB serverB = new ServerB(mediator);

        mediator.setServerA(serverA);
        mediator.setServerB(serverB);

        serverA.sendMessage("ServerA_Port_201");

        System.out.println("------------------------------------");

        serverA.sendMessage("ServerA_Port_200");
    }
}
```

Right click Test.java and then Run as -> Java Application Result:

```
Console ☒                    ■ ✖ ✖ | 🗎 🗎 🗎 🗎 | 🗗 🗔 ▼ 🗂 ▼ ▭ 🗖
<terminated> Test (49) [Java Application] C:\Program Files (x86)\Java\jre6\bin\javaw.exe (202:
ServerB receive message: ServerA_Port_201
ServerB disconnect with ServerA_Port_201
------------------------------------
ServerB receive message: ServerA_Port_200
ServerB connect with ServerA_Port_200 successfully
```

182

Mediator Pattern Case

1. Example: Realize multi-user chat GUI program with UDP protocol.

We add a Server as a mediator. In this star structure, the client computer no longer interacts with another client computer through direct contact; it chat message through the MediatorServer and then MediatorServer broadcast message to all client computer.

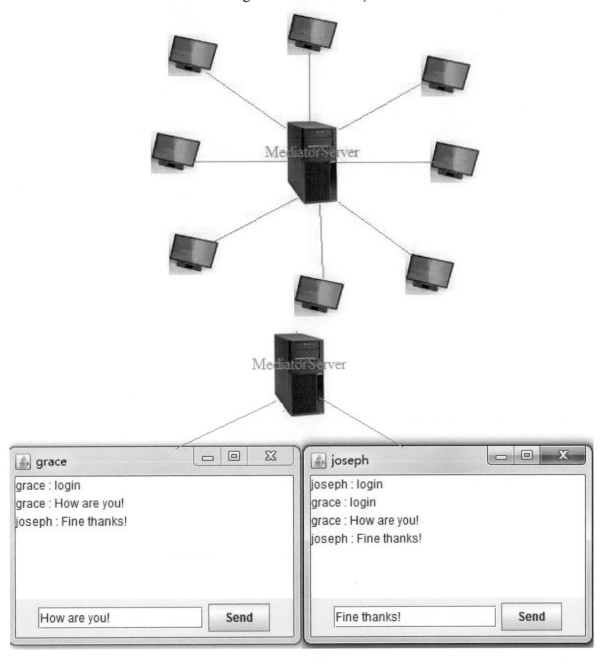

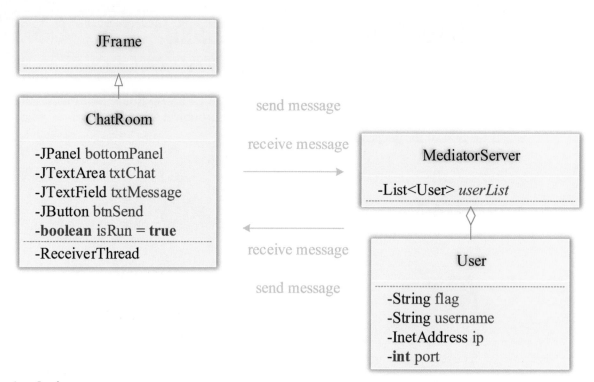

Analysis:

1. The first step is to start MediatorServer, The MediatorServer is listening on port 9001

```java
public class MediatorServer {
    public static void main(String[] args) {
        try {
            DatagramSocket ds = new DatagramSocket(9001);
            while (true) {

            }
        } catch (Exception e) {
            e.printStackTrace();
        }
    }
}
```

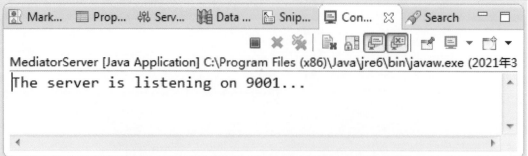

2. Client 1 login with port: 9002, username: joseph and then send JSON message to MediatorServer.
MessageClient.java is tool class to send and read JSON message.

```java
public class TestLogin {
    public static void main(String[] args) {
        Scanner in = new Scanner(System.in);
        System.out.println("Please input port:");
        String port = in.nextLine();

        MessageClient.listen(Integer.parseInt(port));

        System.out.println("Please input login username:");
        String username = in.nextLine();

        String message = "{flag:'login',username:'"+username+"',content:'login'}";
        MessageClient.sendMessage(message); // send JSON message to MediatorServer
    }
}
```

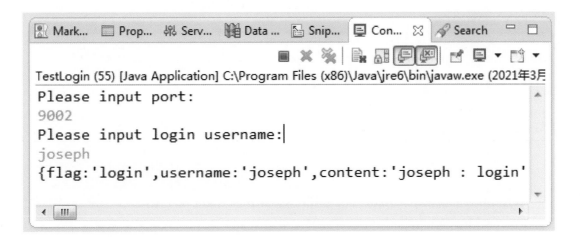

185

3. MediatorServer add this user to userList as online users, MediatorServer broadcast message to all clients

```java
public class MediatorServer {
    public static List<User> userList = new ArrayList<User>(); //online users

    public static void main(String[] args) {
        DatagramSocket ds = new DatagramSocket(9001);
        System.out.println("The server is listening on 9001...");
        while (true) {
            //receive message
            byte[] data = new byte[1024];
            DatagramPacket pack = new DatagramPacket(data, data.length);
            ds.receive(pack);

            String message = new String(data, 0, data.length);
            JSONObject messageJSON = new JSONObject(message);
            String flag = messageJSON.getString("flag");
            String username = messageJSON.getString("username");
            String content = messageJSON.getString("content");

            if ("login".equals(flag)) {
                //save this user to userList as online user
                userList.add(new User(flag, username, pack.getAddress(), pack.getPort()));

                //Broadcast  message
                for (int i = 0; i < userList.size(); i++) {
                    User item = userList.get(i);
                    String msg = "{flag:'login',username:'" + username + "',content:'" + username +
" : login'}";
                    data = msg.getBytes();
                    DatagramPacket dp = new DatagramPacket(data, data.length);
                    dp.setAddress(item.getIp());
                    dp.setPort(item.getPort());
                    ds.send(dp);
                }
            }
        }
    }
}
```

4. All client ChatRoom will receive this message that display on JTextArea txtChat. MessageClient.java is tool class to send and read JSON message.

```java
public class ChatRoom extends JFrame {
    private JPanel bottomPanel;
    private JTextArea txtChat;
    private JTextField txtMessage;
    private JButton btnSend;
    private boolean isRun = true;

    //Receive the message sent by the server
    class ReceiverThread implements Runnable {
        public void run() {
            while (isRun) {
                try {
                    JSONObject messageJSON = MessageClient.receiveMessage();
                    String flag = messageJSON.getString("flag");
                    String username = messageJSON.getString("username");
                    String content = messageJSON.getString("content");

                    txtChat.append(content+"\n");
                } catch (JSONException e) {
                    e.printStackTrace();
                }
            }
        }
    }
}
```

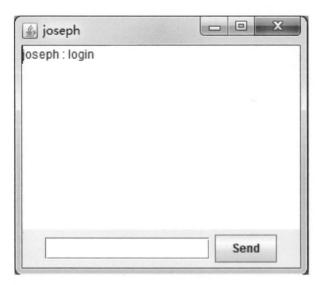

5. Client 2 login with port: 9003, username: grace and then send message to MediatorServer, MediatorServer add this user to userList as online users, MediatorServer broadcast message to all clients, all client ChatRoom will receive this message that display on JTextArea txtChat.

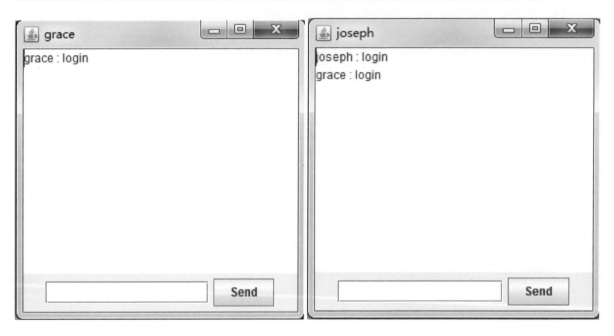

6. All Clients can input message in JTextField txtMessage and click send button to send JSON message to MediatorServer

```
        btnSend = new JButton("Send");
        btnSend.addActionListener(new ActionListener(){
            public void actionPerformed(ActionEvent e) {
                String message =
"{flag:'send',username:'"+ChatRoom.this.getTitle()+"',content:'"+txtMessage.getText()+"'}";
                MessageClient.sendMessage(message);
            }

        });
    }
```

7. MediatorServer receive this message and then broadcast message to all clients

```java
public class MediatorServer {
    public static List<User> userList = new ArrayList<User>();

    public static void main(String[] args) {
        try {
            DatagramSocket ds = new DatagramSocket(9001);
            System.out.println("The server is listening on 9001...");
            while (true) {
                //receive message
                byte[] data = new byte[1024];
                DatagramPacket pack = new DatagramPacket(data, data.length);
                ds.receive(pack);

                String message = new String(data, 0, data.length);
                JSONObject messageJSON = new JSONObject(message);
                String flag = messageJSON.getString("flag");
                String username = messageJSON.getString("username");
                String content = messageJSON.getString("content");

                if ("send".equals(flag)) {
                    //Broadcasst  message
                    for (int i = 0; i < userList.size(); i++) {
                        User item = userList.get(i);
                        String msg = "{flag:'send',username:'" + username + "',content:'" + username +
" : " + content + "'}";
                        data = msg.getBytes();
                        DatagramPacket dp = new DatagramPacket(data, data.length);
                        dp.setAddress(item.getIp());
                        dp.setPort(item.getPort());
                        ds.send(dp);
                    }
                }
            }
        } catch (Exception e) {
            e.printStackTrace();
        }
    }
}
```

8. All client ChatRoom will receive this message that display on JTextArea txtChat.

Create all classes in project test/com.mediator.cases

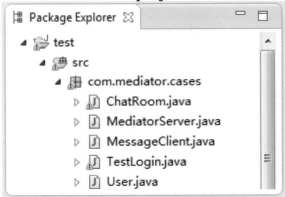

All messages are sent as JSON strings, so first Download the json.jar for parsing JSON strings

http://en.verejava.com/download.jsp?id=1

2. Copy json.jar to test/lib

3. Add json.jar to Referenced Libraries

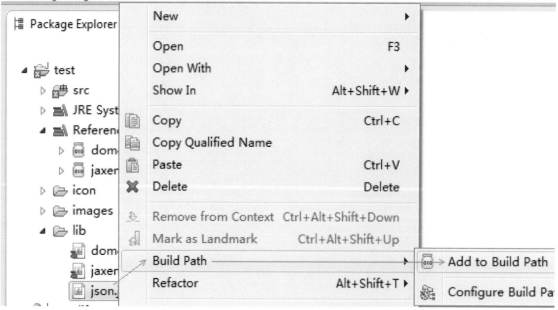

User.java in package com.mediator.cases;

```java
import java.net.InetAddress;
public class User {
    private String flag;
    private String username;
    private InetAddress ip;
    private int port;

    public User(String flag, String username, InetAddress ip, int port) {
        this.flag = flag;
        this.username = username;
        this.ip = ip;
        this.port = port;
    }

    public String getUsername() {
        return username;
    }

    public void setUsername(String username) {
        this.username = username;
    }

    public InetAddress getIp() {
        return ip;
    }

    public void setIp(InetAddress ip) {
        this.ip = ip;
    }

    public int getPort() {
        return port;
    }

    public void setPort(int port) {
        this.port = port;
    }
}
```

MediatorServer.java in package com.mediator.cases;

```java
import java.net.*;
import java.util.*;
import org.json.JSONObject;

public class MediatorServer {
    public static List<User> userList = new ArrayList<User>();

    public static void main(String[] args) {
        try {
            DatagramSocket ds = new DatagramSocket(9001);
            System.out.println("The server is listening on 9001...");
            while (true) {
                //receive message
                byte[] data = new byte[1024];
                DatagramPacket pack = new DatagramPacket(data, data.length);
                ds.receive(pack);

                String message = new String(data, 0, data.length);
                JSONObject messageJSON = new JSONObject(message);
                String flag = messageJSON.getString("flag");
                String username = messageJSON.getString("username");
                String content = messageJSON.getString("content");

                if ("login".equals(flag)) {
                    //save this user to userList as online user
                    userList.add(new User(flag, username, pack.getAddress(), pack.getPort()));

                    //Broadcast  message
                    for (int i = 0; i < userList.size(); i++) {
                        User item = userList.get(i);
                        String msg = "{flag:'login',username:'" + username + "',content:'" + username +
" : login'}";
                        data = msg.getBytes();
                        DatagramPacket dp = new DatagramPacket(data, data.length);
                        dp.setAddress(item.getIp());
                        dp.setPort(item.getPort());
                        ds.send(dp);
                    }
                }
```

```java
            if ("send".equals(flag)) {
              //Broadcasst message
                for (int i = 0; i < userList.size(); i++) {
                    User item = userList.get(i);
                    String msg = "{flag:'send',username:'" + username + "',content:'" + username +
" : " + content + "'}";
                    data = msg.getBytes();
                    DatagramPacket dp = new DatagramPacket(data, data.length);
                    dp.setAddress(item.getIp());
                    dp.setPort(item.getPort());
                    ds.send(dp);
                }
            }
        }
    } catch (Exception e) {
      e.printStackTrace();
    }
  }
}
```

MessageClient.java in package com.mediator.cases;

```java
import java.net.*;
import org.json.JSONObject;
public class MessageClient {
  public static DatagramSocket ds = null;

  public static void listen(int port){
    try {
      ds = new DatagramSocket(port);
    } catch (SocketException e) {
      e.printStackTrace();
    }
  }

  public static void sendMessage(String message){
    try {
      byte[] data = message.getBytes();
      DatagramPacket dp = new DatagramPacket(data, data.length);
      dp.setAddress( InetAddress.getByName("localhost"));
      dp.setPort(9001);
      ds.send(dp);
    } catch (Exception e) {
      e.printStackTrace();
    }
  }

  public static JSONObject receiveMessage(){
    JSONObject messageJSON = null;
    try {
      byte[] data = new byte[1024];
      DatagramPacket pack = new DatagramPacket(data, data.length);
      ds.receive(pack);

      String message = new String(data, 0, data.length);
      System.out.println(message);
      messageJSON = new JSONObject(message);
    } catch (Exception e) {
      e.printStackTrace();
    }
    return messageJSON;
  }
}
```

ChatRoom.java in package com.mediator.cases;

```java
import java.awt.*;
import java.awt.event.*;
import javax.swing.*;
import org.json.*;

public class ChatRoom extends JFrame {
    private JPanel bottomPanel;
    private JTextArea txtChat;
    private JTextField txtMessage;
    private JButton btnSend;
    private boolean isRun = true;

    public ChatRoom() {
        this.setSize(300, 300);
        this.setLayout(new BorderLayout());
        this.setDefaultCloseOperation(EXIT_ON_CLOSE);

        this.add(getTxtChat(), BorderLayout.CENTER);
        this.add(getBottomPanel(), BorderLayout.SOUTH);

        new Thread(new ReceiverThread()).start();
    }

    //Receive the message sent by the server
    class ReceiverThread implements Runnable {
        public void run() {

            while (isRun) {
                try {
                    JSONObject messageJSON = MessageClient.receiveMessage();
                    String flag = messageJSON.getString("flag");
                    String username = messageJSON.getString("username");
                    String content = messageJSON.getString("content");

                    txtChat.append(content+"\n");
                } catch (JSONException e) {
                    e.printStackTrace();
                }
            }
        }
    }
}
```

```java
    public JPanel getBottomPanel() {
        if (bottomPanel == null) {
            bottomPanel = new JPanel();
            bottomPanel.add(getTxtMessage());
            bottomPanel.add(getBtnSend());
        }
        return bottomPanel;
    }

    public JTextArea getTxtChat() {
        if (txtChat == null) {
            txtChat = new JTextArea();
        }
        return txtChat;
    }

    public JTextField getTxtMessage() {
        if (txtMessage == null) {
            txtMessage = new JTextField();
            txtMessage.setColumns(15);
        }
        return txtMessage;
    }

    public JButton getBtnSend() {
        if (btnSend == null) {
            btnSend = new JButton("Send");
            btnSend.addActionListener(new ActionListener(){
                public void actionPerformed(ActionEvent e) {
                    String message =
"{flag:'send',username:'"+ChatRoom.this.getTitle()+"',content:'"+txtMessage.getText()+"'}";
                    MessageClient.sendMessage(message);
                }

            });
        }
        return btnSend;
    }
}
```

TestLogin.java in package com.mediator.cases;

```java
import java.awt.event.*;
import java.net.*;
import java.util.Scanner;
import javax.swing.*;

public class TestLogin {

    public static void main(String[] args) {
        Scanner in = new Scanner(System.in);
        System.out.println("Please input port:");
        String port = in.nextLine();

        MessageClient.listen(Integer.parseInt(port));

        System.out.println("Please input login username:");
        String username = in.nextLine();

        String message = "{flag:'login',username:'"+username+"',content:'login'}";
        MessageClient.sendMessage(message);

        ChatRoom chatRoom = new ChatRoom();
        chatRoom.setVisible(true);
        chatRoom.setTitle(username);
    }
}
```

1. Run As -> Java Application to start MediatorServer.

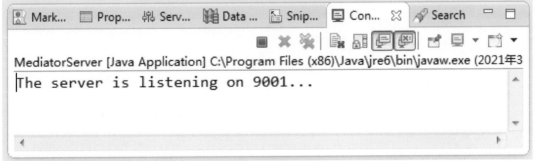

2. Run As -> Java Application to start TestLogin Client 1 **login with port: 9002, username:** joseph **and then send message to** MediatorServer, MediatorServer **add this user to** userList **as online users,** MediatorServer **broadcast message to all clients, all client ChatRoom will receive this message that display on** JTextArea txtChat.

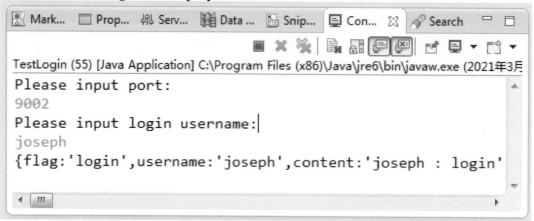

3. Run As -> Java Application to start TestLogin Client 2 **login with port:** 9003, **username:** grace **and then send message to** MediatorServer,MediatorServer **add this user to** userList **as online users,** MediatorServer **broadcast message to all clients, all client ChatRoom will receive this message that display on** JTextArea txtChat.

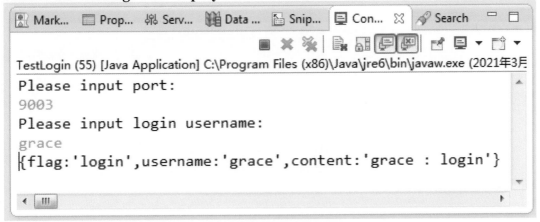

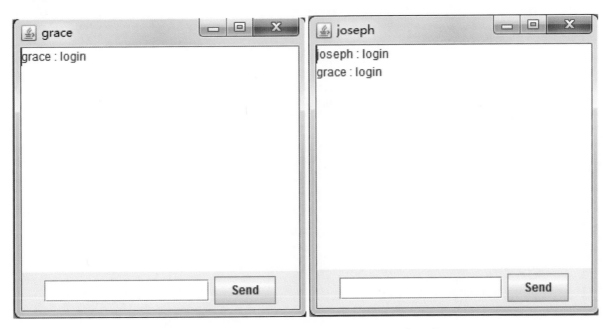

4. All Clients can input message in JTextField txtMessage and click send button to send message to MediatorServer, MediatorServer receive this message and then broadcast message to all clients, all client ChatRoom will receive this message that display on JTextArea txtChat.

In grace chat we input: How are you! And then click send button

In joseph chat we input: Fine thanks! And then click send button

Memento Pattern Principle

Memento Pattern :
Capture the state of an object and save it. The object can be restored from original saved state in the future.

1. Example: Notepad Undo, redo history recovery.

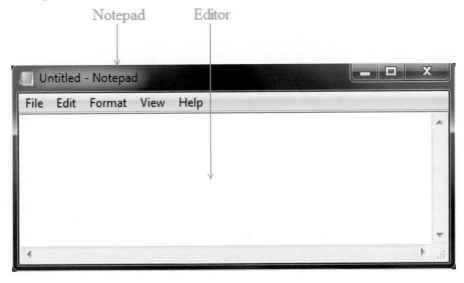

Analysis:
1. Create a class: Memento that as a backup stack for undo and redo.
2. Create a class: Editor that as an editor for text input.
3. Create a class: NotePad that manage Memento.

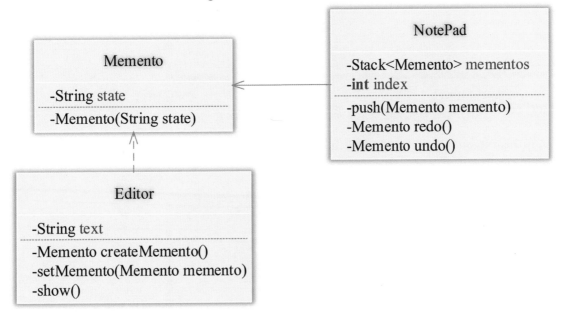

Create a NotePad and a Editor and then input a sentence, at the same time, push this sentence in the backup stack Memento:

Notepad notepad = **new** Notepad();

Editor eidtor = **new** Editor();
eidtor.setState("Move you in the direction of your dream.");
notepad.push(eidtor.createMemento());

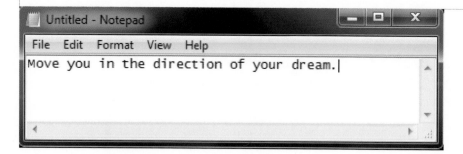

Input anther sentence, at the same time, push this sentence in the backup stack Memento:

eidtor.setState("Ways to start your day positively.");
notepad.push(eidtor.createMemento());

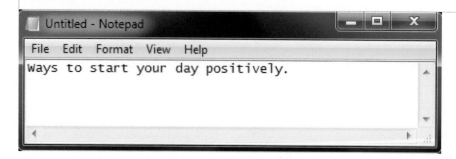

Input anther sentence and then show on Editor:

eidtor.setState("Love can change the world.");
eidtor.show();

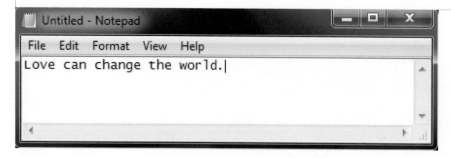

Invoke undo() on NotePad:

```
eidtor.setMemento(notepad.undo());
eidtor.show();
```

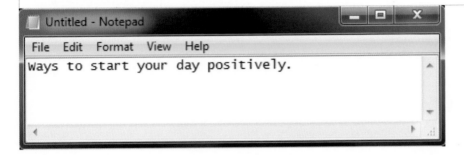

Invoke redo() on NotePad:

```
eidtor.setMemento(notepad.redo());
eidtor.show();
```

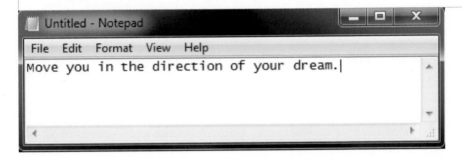

Memento.java in package com.memento.principle;

```java
public class Memento {
    private String state;

    public Memento(String state) {
        super();
        this.state = state;
    }

    public String getState() {
        return state;
    }
}
```

Notepad.java in package com.memento.principle;

```java
import java.util.Stack;

public class Notepad {
    private Stack<Memento> mementos;
    private int index;

    public Notepad() {
        mementos = new Stack<Memento>();
    }

    public void push(Memento memento) {
        mementos.push(memento);
        index++;
    }

    public Memento redo() {
        Memento memento = (Memento) mementos.get(index);
        index++;
        return memento;
    }

    public Memento undo() {
        index--;
        Memento memento = (Memento) mementos.get(index);

        return memento;
    }
}
```

Editor.java in package com.memento.principle;

```java
public class Editor {
    private String text;

    public Editor() {
        super();
    }

    public String getText() {
        return text;
    }

    public void setState(String text) {
        this.text = text;
    }

    public Memento createMemento() {
        return new Memento(text);
    }

    public void setMemento(Memento memento) {
        this.text = memento.getState();
    }

    public void show() {
        System.out.println(text);
    }
}
```

2. Create a Test class : Test.java in package com.memento.principle;

```java
public class Test {
    public static void main(String[] args) {

        Notepad notepad = new Notepad();

        Editor eidtor = new Editor();
        eidtor.setState("Move you in the direction of your dream.");
        notepad.push(eidtor.createMemento());

        eidtor.setState("Ways to start your day positively.");
        notepad.push(eidtor.createMemento());

        eidtor.setState("Love can change the world.");
        eidtor.show();

        //Undo
        eidtor.setMemento(notepad.undo());
        eidtor.show();
        eidtor.setMemento(notepad.undo());
        eidtor.show();

        System.out.println("-----------------------------");

        //Redo
        eidtor.setMemento(notepad.redo());
        eidtor.show();
        eidtor.setMemento(notepad.redo());
        eidtor.show();
    }
}
```

Right click Test.java and then Run as -> Java Application Result:

```
Problems  @ Javadoc  Declaration  Console
Love can change the world.
Ways to start your day positively.
Move you in the direction of your dream.
-------------------------------
Move you in the direction of your dream.
Ways to start your day positively.
```

208

Memento Pattern Case

1. Example: Move the mouse to draw a rectangle on the canvas, and each operation is recorded in memento. Later, press Ctrl+Z and Ctrl+Y to undo and redo

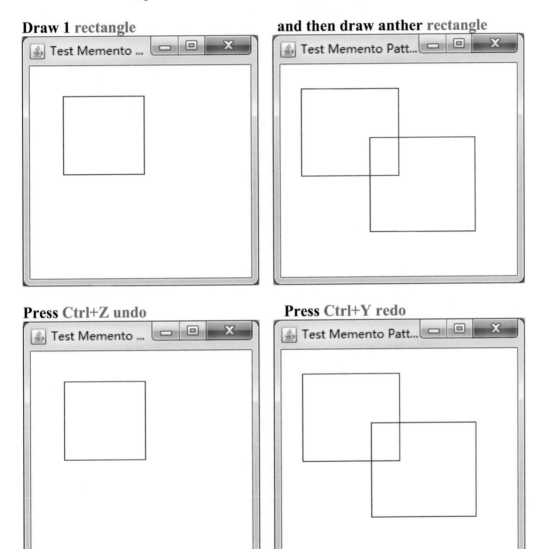

Draw 1 rectangle

and then draw anther rectangle

Press Ctrl+Z undo

Press Ctrl+Y redo

Analysis:

1. Create a class: Rectangle that can draw on canvas.

2. Create a class: Memento that as a backup stack for undo and redo.

3. Create a class: MementoManager that manage Memento.

4. Canvas implements mouse click and move event interfaces: MouseListener, MouseMotionListener.

5. When the mouse is pressed in the event: mousePressed(MouseEvent e), record the pressed x, y coordinates in mousePressedX and mousePressedY

```java
public void mousePressed(MouseEvent e) {
    mousePressedX = e.getX();
    mousePressedY = e.getY();
    mousePressed = true;
}
```

6. When the mouse moves in the event: mouseDragged(MouseEvent e), record the moving x, y coordinates in mouseMovedX and mouseMovedY

```java
public void mouseDragged(MouseEvent e) {
    if(mousePressed){
        mouseMovedX = e.getX();
        mouseMovedY = e.getY();
        drawStatus = 1;
        repaint();
    }
}
```

7. When the mouse is released in the event: mouseReleased(MouseEvent e), record the released x, y coordinates in mouseReleasedX and mouseReleasedY

```java
public void mouseReleased(MouseEvent e) {
    if(drawStatus == 1){
        mouseReleasedX = e.getX();
        mouseReleasedY = e.getY();
        drawStatus = 2;
        repaint();
    }
    mousePressed = false;
}
```

8. Each time the mouse moves and releases, repaint() redraws the rectangle to achieve the rectangle drawing effect.
And back up the result of each drawing rectangle to Memento

```java
protected void paintComponent(Graphics g) {
    super.paintComponent(g);

    if(drawStatus == 1){
        int x = mousePressedX;
        int y = mousePressedY;
        int width = mouseMovedX - mousePressedX;
        int height = mouseMovedY - mousePressedY;
        g.clearRect(x, y, width, height);
        Rectangle rectangle = new Rectangle(x, y, width, height);
        rectangle.draw(g);
    }

    if(drawStatus == 2){
        int x = mousePressedX;
        int y = mousePressedY;
        int width = mouseReleasedX - mousePressedX;
        int height = mouseReleasedY - mousePressedY;
        g.clearRect(x, y, width, height);

        rectList.addFirst(new Rectangle(x, y, width, height));
        MementoManager.push(new Memento((LinkedList<Rectangle>)rectList.clone()));
        drawStatus = 0;
    }

    for(int i=0;i<rectList.size();i++){
        Rectangle rectangle = rectList.get(i);
        rectangle.draw(g);
    }
}
```

9. Canvas implements key pressed event interfaces: KeyListener.

10. Press Ctrl+Z and Ctrl+Y to achieve undo and redo function.

```java
public void keyPressed(KeyEvent e) {
    int keyCode = e.getKeyCode();
    if(e.isControlDown() && keyCode == KeyEvent.VK_Z){
        if(!MementoManager.isEmpty()){
            Memento memento = MementoManager.undo();
            if(memento!=null){
                rectList = memento.getState();
                repaint();
            }
        }
    }else  if(e.isControlDown() && keyCode == KeyEvent.VK_Y){
        if(!MementoManager.isEmpty()){
            Memento memento = MementoManager.redo();
            if(memento!=null){
                rectList = memento.getState();
                repaint();
            }
        }
    }
}
```

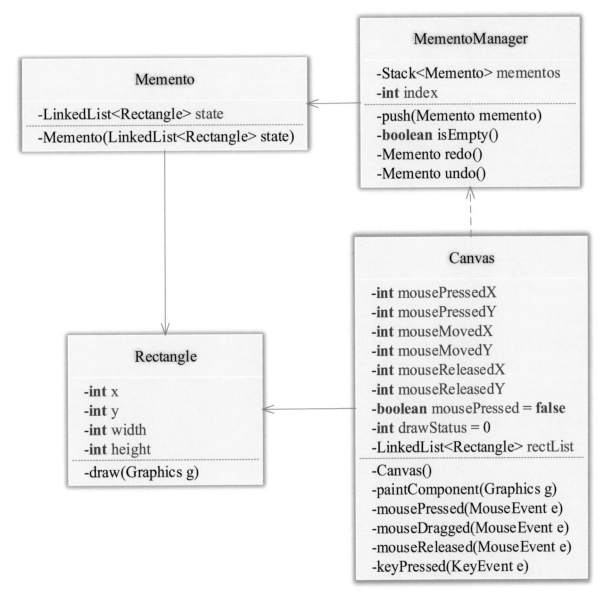

Create all classes in project test/com.memento.cases

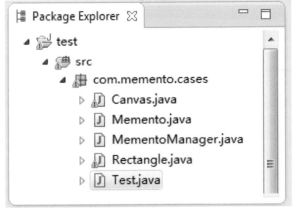

Rectangle.java in package com.memento.cases;

```java
import java.awt.*;
import java.awt.image.BufferedImage;

public  class Rectangle  implements Cloneable{
   protected int x;
   protected int y;
   protected int width;
   protected int height;

   public Rectangle(int x, int y, int width, int height){
      this.x = x;
      this.y = y;
      this.width = width;
      this.height = height;
   }

   public void draw(Graphics g){
       g.drawRect(this.x, this.y, this.width, this.height);
   }

   public void setX(int x) {
      this.x = x;
   }

   public void setY(int y) {
      this.y = y;
   }

   protected Object clone() {
      try {
        return super.clone();
      } catch (CloneNotSupportedException e) {
        e.printStackTrace();
      }
      return null;
   }
}
```

Memento.java in package com.memento.cases;

```java
import java.util.LinkedList;

public class Memento {
    private LinkedList<Rectangle> state;

    public Memento(LinkedList<Rectangle> state) {
        this.state = state;
    }

    public LinkedList<Rectangle> getState() {
        return state;
    }
}
```

MementoManager.java in package com.memento.cases;

```java
import java.util.Stack;

public class MementoManager {
    private static Stack<Memento> mementos = new Stack<Memento>();
    private static int index = -1;

    public static void push(Memento memento) {
        mementos.push(memento);
        index++;
    }

    public static boolean isEmpty(){
        return mementos.isEmpty();
    }

    public static Memento redo() {
        if(index>= mementos.size()){
            return null;
        }

        Memento memento = (Memento) mementos.get(index);
        index++;
        return memento;
    }
```

```java
    public static Memento undo() {
      if(index<=0){
        return null;
      }
      index--;
      Memento memento = (Memento) mementos.get(index);

      return memento;
    }
}
```

Canvas.java **in package** com.memento.cases;

```java
import java.awt.*;
import java.awt.event.*;
import java.awt.image.BufferedImage;
import java.io.*;
import java.util.*;
import javax.imageio.ImageIO;
import javax.swing.*;

public class Canvas extends JPanel implements MouseListener,
MouseMotionListener,KeyListener {
  private int mousePressedX;
  private int mousePressedY;
  private int mouseMovedX;
  private int mouseMovedY;
  private int mouseReleasedX;
  private int mouseReleasedY;
  private boolean mousePressed = false;
  private int drawStatus = 0;
  private LinkedList<Rectangle> rectList = new LinkedList<Rectangle>();

  public Canvas() {
    this.setLayout(null);
    this.setBackground(Color.WHITE);
    this.requestFocus();

    this.addMouseMotionListener(this);
    this.addMouseListener(this);
    this.addKeyListener(this);
  }
```

```java
protected void paintComponent(Graphics g) {
  super.paintComponent(g);
  if(drawStatus == 1){
    int x = mousePressedX;
    int y = mousePressedY;
    int width = mouseMovedX - mousePressedX;
    int height = mouseMovedY - mousePressedY;
    g.clearRect(x, y, width, height);
    Rectangle rectangle = new Rectangle(x, y, width, height);
    rectangle.draw(g);
  }

  if(drawStatus == 2){
    int x = mousePressedX;
    int y = mousePressedY;
    int width = mouseReleasedX - mousePressedX;
    int height = mouseReleasedY - mousePressedY;
    g.clearRect(x, y, width, height);

    rectList.addFirst(new Rectangle(x, y, width, height));
    MementoManager.push(new Memento((LinkedList<Rectangle>)rectList.clone()));
    drawStatus = 0;
  }

  for(int i=0;i<rectList.size();i++){
    Rectangle rectangle = rectList.get(i);
    rectangle.draw(g);
  }
}

public void mousePressed(MouseEvent e) {
  mousePressedX = e.getX();
  mousePressedY = e.getY();
  mousePressed = true;
}

public void mouseDragged(MouseEvent e) {
  if(mousePressed){
    mouseMovedX = e.getX();
    mouseMovedY = e.getY();
    drawStatus = 1;
    repaint();
  }
}
```

```java
@Override
public void mouseReleased(MouseEvent e) {
    if(drawStatus == 1){
        mouseReleasedX = e.getX();
        mouseReleasedY = e.getY();
        drawStatus = 2;
        repaint();
    }
    mousePressed = false;
}

@Override
public void keyPressed(KeyEvent e) {
    int keyCode = e.getKeyCode();
    if(e.isControlDown() && keyCode == KeyEvent.VK_Z){
        if(!MementoManager.isEmpty()){
            Memento memento = MementoManager.undo();
            if(memento!=null){
                rectList = memento.getState();
                repaint();
            }
        }
    }else  if(e.isControlDown() && keyCode == KeyEvent.VK_Y){
        if(!MementoManager.isEmpty()){
            Memento memento = MementoManager.redo();
            if(memento!=null){
                rectList = memento.getState();
                repaint();
            }
        }
    }
}

@Override
public void mouseClicked(MouseEvent e) {

}

@Override
public void mouseMoved(MouseEvent e) {

}
```

```java
    @Override
    public void mouseEntered(MouseEvent e) {

    }

    @Override
    public void mouseExited(MouseEvent e) {

    }

    @Override
    public void keyTyped(KeyEvent e) {

    }

    @Override
    public void keyReleased(KeyEvent e) {

    }
}
```

Test.java in package com.memento.cases;

```java
import java.awt.*;
import javax.swing.*;

public class Test {
    private static Canvas canvas;

    public static void main(String[] args) {
        JFrame frame = new JFrame("Test Memento Pattern Case");
        canvas = new Canvas();
        frame.add(canvas, BorderLayout.CENTER);
        frame.setSize(500, 300);
        frame.setVisible(true);
        frame.setDefaultCloseOperation(JFrame.EXIT_ON_CLOSE);
        frame.setFocusable(false);
        canvas.requestFocus();
    }
}
```

Right click Test.java **and then** Run as -> Java Application **Result:**

Draw 1 rectangle

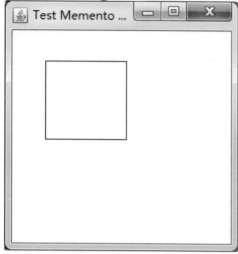

and then draw anther rectangle

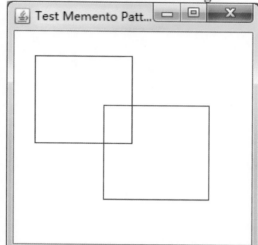

Press Ctrl+Z undo

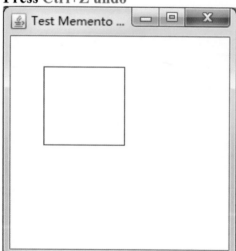

Press Ctrl+Y redo

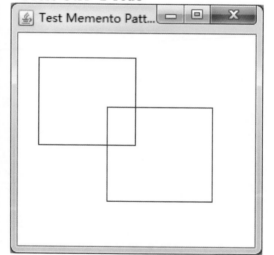

Observer Pattern Principle

Observer Pattern : Define a one-to-many dependency between objects so that when one object changes state, all its dependents are notified and updated automatically.

The Model-View-Controller (MVC) is an architectural pattern that separates an application into three main logical components: the model, the view, and the controller. Each of these components are built to handle specific development aspects of an application.

Observer and Observable
The Java language supports the MVC architecture with two classes:

Observer: Any object that wishes to be notified when the state of another object changes.
   update(Observable obs, Object obj): Called when a change has occurred in the state of the observable.
Observable: Any object whose state may be of interest, and in whom another object may register an interest.
   addObserver(Observer obs): Adds an observer to the internal list of observers.
   setChanged():Sets the internal flag that indicates this observable has changed state.
   notifyObservers():Checks the internal flag to see if the observable has changed state and notifies all observers.

1. Example: In the stock market, stock data changes at any time. Sellers and buyers can see the changes at the same time.

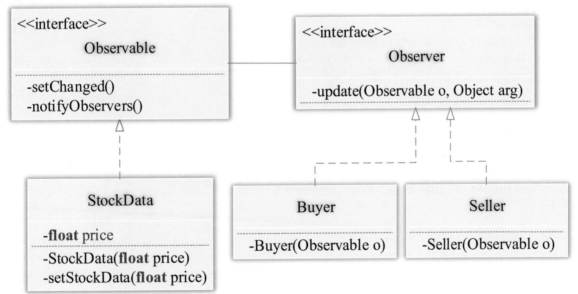

StockData.java in package com.observer.principle;

```java
import java.util.*;
public class StockData extends Observable {
  private float price;

  public StockData(float price) {
    this.price = price;
  }

  public float getPrice() {
    return price;
  }

  public void setStockData(float price) {
    this.price = price;
    setChanged();
    notifyObservers();
  }
}
```

Buyer.java in package com.observer.principle;

```java
import java.util.*;
public class Buyer implements Observer{
  public Buyer(Observable o){
    o.addObserver(this);
  }

  public void update(Observable o, Object arg){
    if(o instanceof StockData){
      StockData data=(StockData)o;
      System.out.println("Buyer Price:"+data.getPrice());
    }
  }
}
```

Seller.java in package com.observer.principle;

```java
import java.util.*;
public class Seller implements Observer{
    public Seller(Observable o){
        o.addObserver(this);
    }

    public void update(Observable o, Object arg){
        if(o instanceof StockData){
            StockData data=(StockData)o;
            System.out.println("Seller Price:"+data.getPrice());
        }
    }
}
```

2. Create a Test class : TestObserver.java in package com.observer.principle;

```java
public class TestObserver {
    public static void main(String[] args) {
        StockData data = new StockData(16.9f);

        Buyer buyer = new Buyer(data);
        Seller seller = new Seller(data);

        data.setStockData(18.9f);

        System.out.println("----------------------");

        data.setStockData(12.9f);
    }
}
```

Right click TestObserver.java and then Run as -> Java Application Result:

```
Markers   Prope...   Servers   Data S...   Snipp...   Cons...   Search

Seller Price:18.9
Buyer Price:18.9
----------------------
Seller Price:12.9
Buyer Price:12.9
```

Observer Pattern Case

Example: producer and consumer models.

The producer and consumer problem is one of the small collection of standard, well-known problems in concurrent programming. A queue buffer and two classes of threads, producers and consumers put items into the queue buffer(producers) and take items out of the queue buffer(consumers).

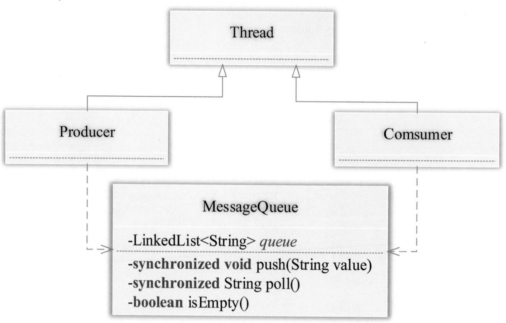

MessageQueue.java in package com.observer.cases;

```java
import java.util.LinkedList;
public class MessageQueue {
    private static LinkedList<String> queue = new LinkedList<String>();

    public static synchronized void push(String value) {
        queue.push(value);
    }

    public static synchronized String poll() {
        return queue.poll();
    }

    public static boolean isEmpty() {
        return queue.isEmpty();
    }
}
```

Producer.java in package com.observer.cases;

```java
public class Producer extends Thread {

    public void run() {
        for (int i = 0; i < 10; i++) {
            String message = "New Message : " + i;
            MessageQueue.push(message); //push message to queue buffer
        }
    }
}
```

Comsumer.java in package com.observer.cases;

```java
public class Comsumer extends Thread {
    public static boolean isRun = true;

    public void run() {
        while (isRun) {
            if (!MessageQueue.isEmpty()) {
                String message = MessageQueue.poll();//get message from queue buffer
                System.out.println(message);
            }

            try {
                Thread.sleep(1000);
            } catch (InterruptedException e) {
                e.printStackTrace();
            }
        }
    }
}
```

2. Create a Test class : TestMessageQueue.java in package com.observer.cases;

```java
public class TestMessageQueue {

    public static void main(String[] args) {

        //start producer thread push message to queue buffer
        new Producer().start();

        //start comsumer thread get message from queue buffer
        new Comsumer().start();
    }
}
```

Right click TestMessageQueue.java and then Run as -> Java Application Result:

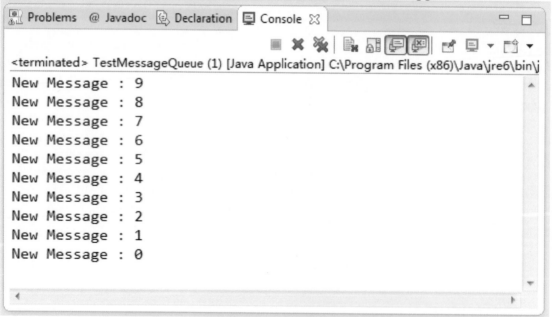

Visitor Pattern Principle

Visitor Pattern : lets you define a new operation without changing the classes of the elements on which it operates.

1. Example: WebServer can attach more website service and can accept various types of visitors to visit the website ,Visitors visit e-business websites and video websites have different requirements.

    Visitor1 visit e-business websites want to buy books
    Visitor1 visit video websites want to watch a movie
    Visitor2 visit e-business websites want to write a review
    Visitor2 visit video websites want to download a movie

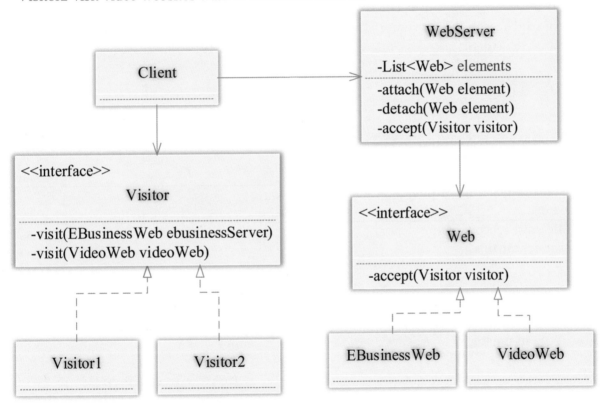

Web.java in package com.visitor.principle;

```java
public interface Web {

    void accept(Visitor visitor);
}
```

EBusinessWeb.java in package com.visitor.principle;

```java
public class EBusinessWeb implements Web {

    public void accept(Visitor visitor) {
        visitor.visit(this);
    }
}
```

VideoWeb.java in package com.visitor.principle;

```java
public class VideoWeb implements Web {

    public void accept(Visitor visitor) {
        visitor.visit(this);
    }
}
```

Visitor.java in package com.visitor.principle;

```java
public interface Visitor {

    public void visit(EBusinessWeb ebusinessServer);

    public void visit(VideoWeb videoWeb);
}
```

Visitor1.java in package com.visitor.principle;

```java
public class Visitor1 implements Visitor{
    public void visit(EBusinessWeb ebusinessServer){
        System.out.println("I want to buy books");
    }

    public void visit(VideoWeb videoWeb){
        System.out.println("I want to watch a movie");
    }
}
```

Visitor2.java in package com.visitor.principle;

```java
public class Visitor2 implements Visitor{
    public void visit(EBusinessWeb ebusinessServer){
        System.out.println("I want to write a review");
    }

    public void visit(VideoWeb videoWeb){
        System.out.println("I want to download a movie");
    }
}
```

WebServer.java in package com.visitor.principle;

```java
import java.util.*;
public class WebServer {
    private List<Web> elements = new ArrayList<Web>();

    public void attach(Web element) {
        elements.add(element);
    }

    public void detach(Web element) {
        elements.remove(elements);
    }

    public void accept(Visitor visitor) {
        for (Web web : elements) {
            web.accept(visitor);
        }
    }
}
```

2. Create a Test class : TestVisitor.java in package com.visitor.principle;

```java
public class TestVisitor {

    public static void main(String[] args) {

        WebServer webServer = new WebServer();

        webServer.attach(new EBusinessWeb());
        webServer.attach(new VideoWeb());

        Visitor visitor1 = new Visitor1();
        webServer.accept(visitor1);

        System.out.println("------------------------");

        Visitor visitor2 = new Visitor2();
        webServer.accept(visitor2);
    }
}
```

Right click TestVisitor.java **and then** Run as -> Java Application **Result:**

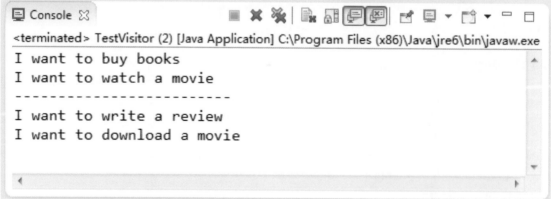

Visitor Pattern Case

1. Example: When the mouse move over to visit the plane and the enemy plane, the message of tips description(attack power) of the plane and description(defense power) of the enemy plane are displayed on title.

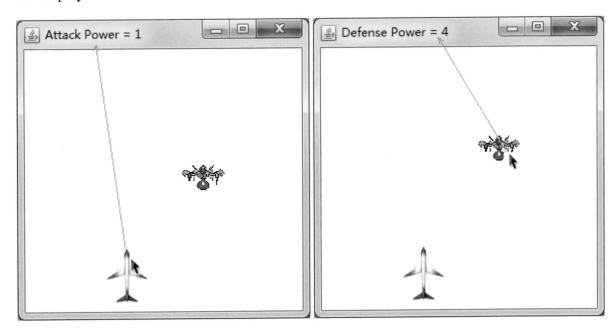

Analysis:
1. Create an abstract class: Sprite implements basic drawing and moving functions
2. Create 2 class: Enemy, Plane inherit from Sprite.
   Enemy has attribute:defensePower = 4
   Plane has attribute: attackPower = 1
3. All Enemy and Plane are added to List<Sprite> spriteList

```
public Canvas() {
    this.setLayout(null);
    this.setBackground(Color.WHITE);

    plane = new Plane(80, 200, "images/red_plane.png");
    enemy = new Enemy(160, 20,"images/enemy.png");

    spriteList.add(plane);
    spriteList.add(enemy);
}
```

4. Enemy move down

```java
protected void paintComponent(Graphics g) {
    super.paintComponent(g);

    plane.draw(g);
    enemy.draw(g);
    enemy.move(0, 3);
}
```

4. Canvas implements key event: KeyListener. Press up,down,left, right key to move.

```java
public void keyPressed(KeyEvent e) {
    int keyCode = e.getKeyCode();
    if(keyCode == KeyEvent.VK_UP){
        plane.move(0, -3);
    }else if(keyCode == KeyEvent.VK_DOWN){
        plane.move(0, 3);
    }else if(keyCode == KeyEvent.VK_RIGHT){
        plane.move(3, 0);
    }else if(keyCode ==  KeyEvent.VK_LEFT){
        plane.move(-3, 0);
    }
}
```

5. Canvas implements mouse move event: MouseMotionListener

6. When the mouse move over to visit the plane and the enemy plane, the message of tips attack power of the plane and defense power of the enemy plane are displayed on title.

```java
public void mouseMoved(MouseEvent e) {
    int x = e.getX();
    int y = e.getY();

    for(int i=0;i<spriteList.size();i++){
        Sprite sprite = spriteList.get(i);
        if(sprite.contains(x, y)){
            sprite.accept(new VisitorDisplay());
        }
    }
}
```

UML Diagram:

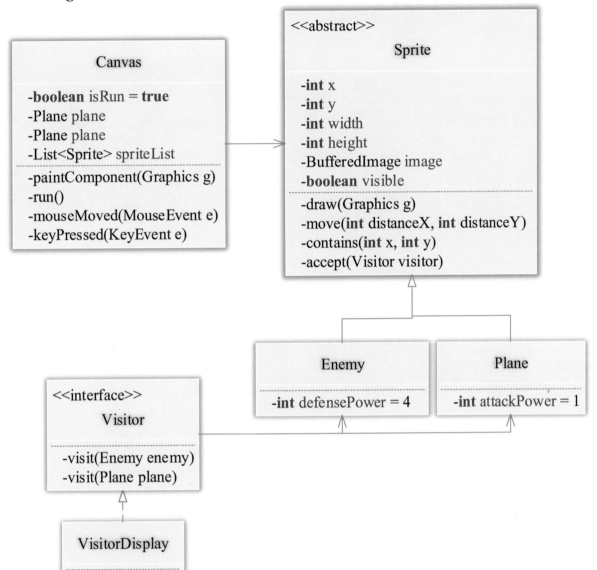

Create all classes in project test/com.visitor.cases

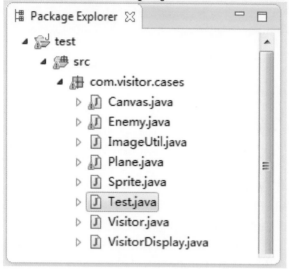

Copy ImageUtil.java **code here from the previous chapter:** Animation

Sprite.java **in package** com.visitor.cases;

```java
import java.awt.Graphics;
import java.awt.image.BufferedImage;

abstract class Sprite {
    protected int x; // x coordinate of Canvas
    protected int y; // y coordinate of Canvas
    protected int width;
    protected int height;
    protected BufferedImage image;
    protected boolean visible;

    public Sprite(int x, int y, String imagePath){
        this.x = x;
        this.y = y;
        this.image=ImageUtil.loadImage(imagePath);
        this.width = this.image.getWidth();
        this.height = this.image.getHeight();
    }

    public void draw(Graphics g){
        g.drawImage(image, this.x, this.y, null);
    }
}
```

```java
public void move(int distanceX, int distanceY){
    this.x = this.x + distanceX;
    this.y = this.y + distanceY;
}

public boolean contains(int x, int y){
    if((x > this.x && x - this.x < width) && (y > this.y && y - this.y < height)){
        return true;
    }
    return false;
}

public abstract void accept(Visitor visitor);

public int getWidth() {
    return width;
}
public int getHeight() {
    return height;
}

public int getX() {
    return x;
}
public void setX(int x) {
    this.x = x;
}

public int getY() {
    return y;
}
public void setY(int y) {
    this.y = y;
}

public boolean isVisible() {
    return visible;
}

public void setVisible(boolean visible) {
    this.visible = visible;
}
}
```

Plane.java in package com.visitor.cases;

```java
import java.awt.image.BufferedImage;
public class Plane  extends Sprite{
   private int attackPower = 1;

   public Plane(int x, int y, String imagePath) {
      super(x, y, imagePath);
   }

   public void accept(Visitor visitor) {
      visitor.visit(this);
   }
   public int getAttackPower() {
      return attackPower;
   }
}
```

Enemy.java in package com.visitor.cases;

```java
import java.awt.image.BufferedImage;
public class Enemy  extends Sprite{
   private int defensePower = 4;

   public Enemy(int x, int y, String imagePath) {
      super(x, y, imagePath);
   }

   public void move(int distanceX, int distanceY){
      this.x = this.x + distanceX;
      this.y = this.y + distanceY;
      if(this.y + this.height <=0){
         this.setVisible(false);
      }
   }

   public void accept(Visitor visitor) {
      visitor.visit(this);
   }
   public int getDefensePower() {
      return defensePower;
   }
}
```

Visitor.java in package com.visitor.cases;

```java
public interface Visitor {

  public void visit(Enemy enemy);

  public void visit(Plane plane);
}
```

VisitorDisplay.java in package com.visitor.cases;

```java
public  class VisitorDisplay implements Visitor{

  public void visit(Enemy enemy){
    Test.frame.setTitle("Defense Power = " + enemy.getDefensePower());
  }

  public void visit(Plane plane){
    Test.frame.setTitle("Attack Power = " + plane.getAttackPower());
  }
}
```

Canvas.java in package com.visitor.cases;

```java
import java.awt.*;
import java.awt.event.*;
import java.util.*;
import javax.swing.JPanel;

public class Canvas extends JPanel implements Runnable, MouseMotionListener,
KeyListener{
  private boolean isRun = true;
  private Plane plane;
  private Enemy enemy;
  private java.util.List<Sprite> spriteList = new ArrayList<Sprite>();

  public Canvas() {
    this.setLayout(null);
    this.setBackground(Color.WHITE);

    plane = new Plane(80, 200, "images/red_plane.png");
    enemy = new Enemy(160, 20,"images/enemy.png");
```

```java
    spriteList.add(plane);
    spriteList.add(enemy);

    this.addMouseMotionListener(this);
    this.addKeyListener(this);

    new Thread(this).start();
}

protected void paintComponent(Graphics g) {
    super.paintComponent(g);

    plane.draw(g);
    enemy.draw(g);
    enemy.move(0, 3);
}

public void run() {
    while(isRun){
        try {
            Thread.sleep(200);
            Canvas.this.repaint();
        } catch (InterruptedException e) {
            e.printStackTrace();
        }
    }
}

public void mouseDragged(MouseEvent e) {

}
public void mouseMoved(MouseEvent e) {
    int x = e.getX();
    int y = e.getY();

    for(int i=0;i<spriteList.size();i++){
        Sprite sprite = spriteList.get(i);
        if(sprite.contains(x, y)){
            sprite.accept(new VisitorDisplay());
        }
    }
}
```

```java
public void keyPressed(KeyEvent e) {
    int keyCode = e.getKeyCode();
    if(keyCode == KeyEvent.VK_UP){
        plane.move(0, -3);
    }else if(keyCode == KeyEvent.VK_DOWN){
        plane.move(0, 3);
    }else if(keyCode == KeyEvent.VK_RIGHT){
        plane.move(3, 0);
    }else if(keyCode ==  KeyEvent.VK_LEFT){
        plane.move(-3, 0);
    }
}

public void keyTyped(KeyEvent e) {

}

@Override
public void keyReleased(KeyEvent e) {

}
}
```

Create a test class: Test.java in package com.visitor.cases;

```java
import java.awt.BorderLayout;
import javax.swing.JFrame;

public class Test {
    public static JFrame frame;

    public static void main(String[] args) {
        frame = new JFrame("Design Pattern Visitor");
        Canvas canvas = new Canvas();
        frame.add(canvas, BorderLayout.CENTER);
        frame.setSize(300, 300);
        canvas.setFocusable(true);
        frame.setVisible(true);
        canvas.requestFocus();
    }
}
```

Right click Test.java **and then** Run as -> Java Application

When the mouse move over to visit the plane and the enemy plane, the message of tips description(attack power) of the plane and description(defense power) of the enemy plane are displayed on title.

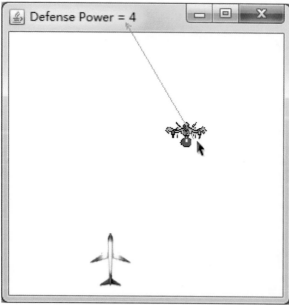

State Pattern Principle

State Pattern : In a variety of states, a manager determines the different needs of the customer's in different states

Example : The Flow for a process in the company will go through different states: Apply, Verify, Approve etc.

Analysis:

1. Create an interface: State and then create 1 method: handle(Flow flow) to deal with the state.
2. Create 3 implementations class: ApplyState, VerifyState, ApproveState,
3. Create an class: Flow to set state and handle current state.

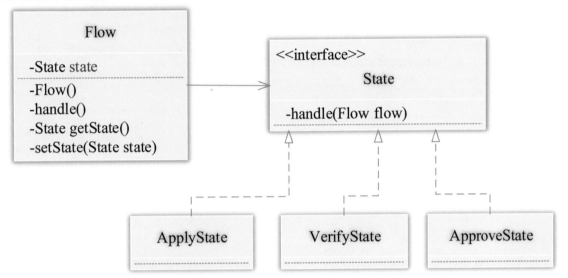

State.java in package com.state.principle;

```
public interface State {
    public void handle(Flow flow);
}
```

ApplyState.java in package com.state.principle;

```
public class ApplyState implements State {

    public void handle(Flow flow) {
        System.out.println("The current state is Apply.");
        flow.setState(new VerifyState());
    }
}
```

VerifyState.java in package com.state.principle;

```java
public class VerifyState implements State {

    public void handle(Flow flow) {
        System.out.println("The current state is Verify.");
        flow.setState(new ApproveState());
    }
}
```

ApproveState.java in package com.state.principle;

```java
public class ApproveState implements State {

    public void handle(Flow flow) {
        System.out.println("The current state is Approve.");
        flow.setState(new ApplyState ());
    }
}
```

Flow.java in package com.state.principle;

```java
public class Flow {
    private State state;

    public Flow() {
        //Define the initial state of the environment
        this.state = new ApplyState();
    }

    //Process the request
    public void handle() {
        state.handle(this);
    }

    public State getState() {
        return state;
    }

    public void setState(State state) {
        this.state = state;
    }
}
```

. **Create a Test class : Test.java in package com.state.principle;**

```java
public class Test {

    public static void main(String[] args) {
        Flow flow = new Flow();
        flow.handle();
        flow.handle();
        flow.handle();
    }
}
```

Right click Test.java and then Run as -> Java Application Result:

```
Console ☒
<terminated> Test (51) [Java Application] C:\Program Files (x86)\Java\jre6\bin\javaw.exe (202:
The current state is Apply.
The current state is Verify.
The current state is Approve.
The current state is Apply.
```

State Pattern Case

1. In the game, the background change on canvas from one state to anther state. different levels show different backgrounds

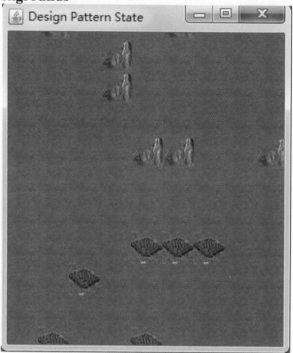

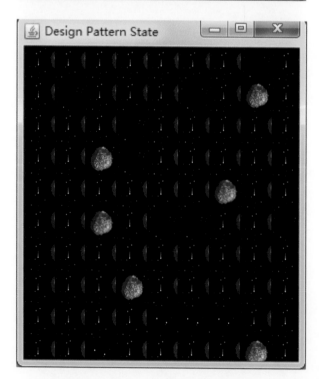

TiledLayer:

A TiledLayer is a visual element composed of a grid of cells that can be filled with a set of tile images. This class allows large virtual layers to be created without the need for an extremely large Image. This technique is commonly used in 2D gaming platforms to create very large backgrounds

Tiles:

The tiles used to fill the TiledLayer's cells are provided in a single Image object. The Image is broken up into a series of equally-sized tiles; the tile size is specified along with the Image. As shown in the figure below, the same tile set can be stored in several different arrangements depending on what is the most convenient for the game developer.

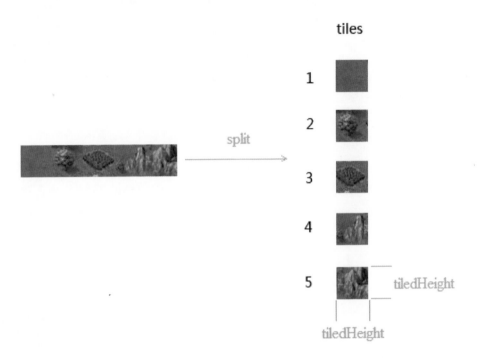

Each tile is assigned a unique index number. The tile located in the upper-left corner of the Image is assigned an index of 1. The remaining tiles are then numbered consecutively in row-major order (indices are assigned across the first row, then the second row, and so on).

Cells

The TiledLayer's grid is made up of equally sized cells; the number of rows and columns in the grid are specified in the constructor, and the physical size of the cells is defined by the size of the tiles. The contents of each cell is specified by means of a tile index;

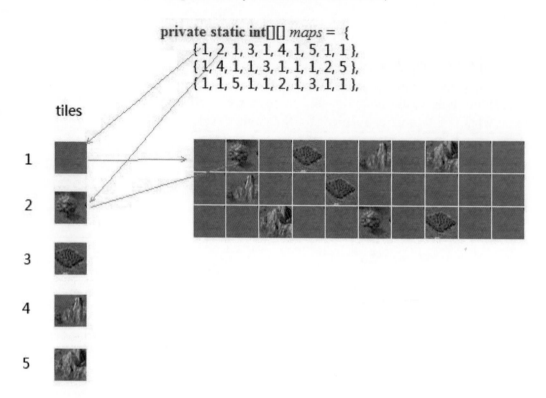

```
private static int[][] maps = {
    { 1, 2, 1, 3, 1, 4, 1, 5, 1, 1 },
    { 1, 4, 1, 1, 3, 1, 1, 1, 2, 5 },
    { 1, 1, 5, 1, 1, 2, 1, 3, 1, 1 },
```

private static int[][] *maps* = {
    { 1, 2, 1, 3, 1, 4, 1, 5, 1, 1 },
    { 1, 4, 1, 1, 3, 1, 1, 1, 2, 5 },
    { 1, 1, 5, 1, 1, 2, 1, 3, 1, 1 },

tiles

1

2

3

4

5

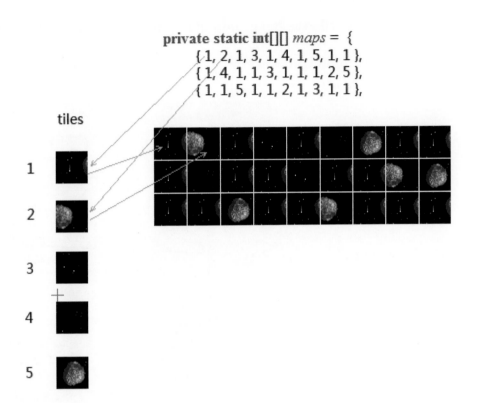

Use a two-dimensional array to clip the image into tiles and spread it on the background

setClip(int x, int y, int width, int height): Sets the current clip to the rectangle specified by the given coordinates.

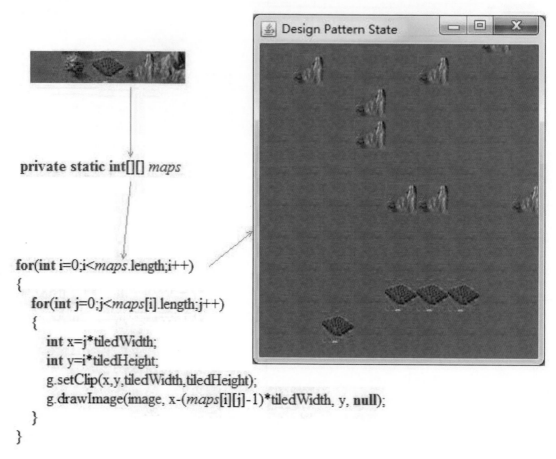

```
private static int[][] maps

for(int i=0;i<maps.length;i++)
{
    for(int j=0;j<maps[i].length;j++)
    {
        int x=j*tiledWidth;
        int y=i*tiledHeight;
        g.setClip(x,y,tiledWidth,tiledHeight);
        g.drawImage(image, x-(maps[i][j]-1)*tiledWidth, y, null);
    }
}
```

Analysis:
1. Create an abstract class: TiledLayer is a visual element composed of a grid of cells that can be filled with a set of tile images.
2. Create 2 implementations class: MapLayer, Map2Layer to achieve different levels show different backgrounds
3. Create a class: MapContext and then create a method: addMap(TiledLayer tiledLayer) to add MapLayer, Map2Layer to LinkedList<TiledLayer> tiledLayerList.
   Create a method: next() to realize the conversion of the state of 2 maps MapLayer, Map2Layer.

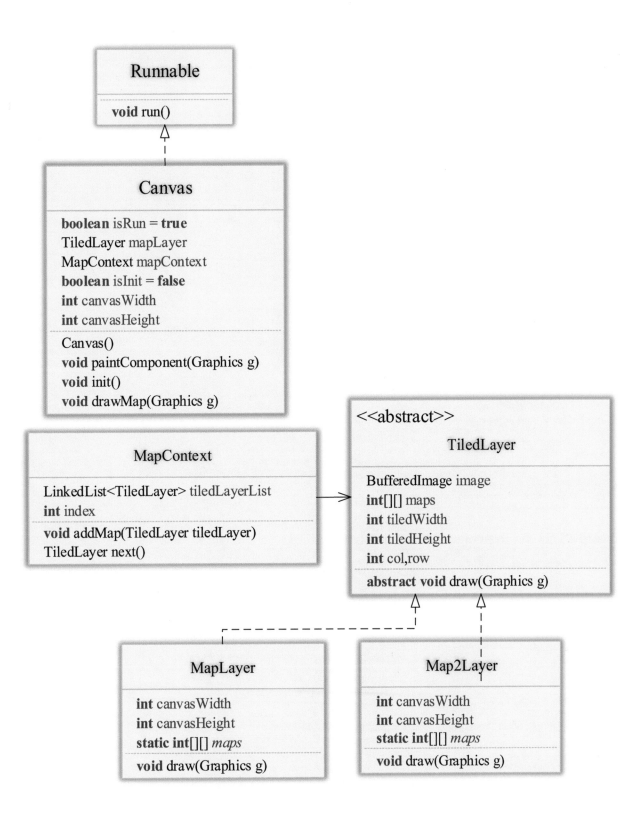

Copy map.png, map2.png to project test/images

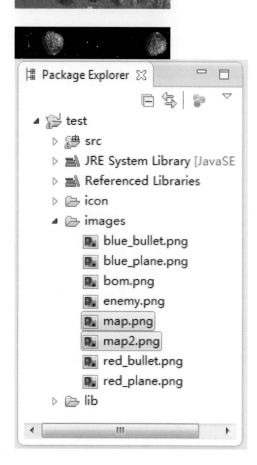

Create all classes in project test/com.state.cases

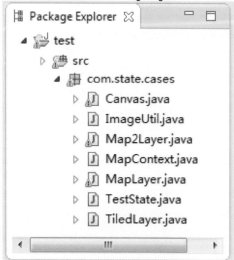

Copy ImageUtil.java code here from the previous chapter: Animation

TiledLayer:

BufferedImage image: the Image to use for creating the tile set.
int tiledWidth: the width in pixels of a single tile.
int tiledHeight: the height in pixels of a single tile.
int row: the height of the TiledLayer, expressed as a number of cells.
int col: the width of the TiledLayer, expressed as a number of cells.

TiledLayer.java in package com.state.cases;

```java
import java.awt.Graphics;
import java.awt.image.BufferedImage;

public abstract class TiledLayer {

    protected BufferedImage image;
    protected int[][] maps;
    protected int tiledWidth;
    protected int tiledHeight;
    protected int col,row;

    public TiledLayer(String imagePath, int[][] maps, int tiledWidth,int tiledHeight, int col,
int row) {
        this.image = ImageUtil.loadImage(imagePath);
        this.maps = maps;
        this.tiledWidth = tiledWidth;
        this.tiledHeight = tiledHeight;
        this.col = col;
        this.row = row;
    }

    public abstract void draw(Graphics g);

    public int[][] getMaps() {
        return maps;
    }

    public void setMaps(int[][] maps) {
        this.maps = maps;
    }
```

```java
public int getTiledWidth() {
    return tiledWidth;
}

public void setTiledWidth(int tiledWidth) {
    this.tiledWidth = tiledWidth;
}

public int getTiledHeight() {
    return tiledHeight;
}

public void setTiledHeight(int tiledHeight) {
    this.tiledHeight = tiledHeight;
}

public int getCol() {
    return col;
}

public void setCol(int col) {
    this.col = col;
}

public int getRow() {
    return row;
}

public void setRow(int row) {
    this.row = row;
}
}
```

```java
import java.awt.*;
import java.awt.image.BufferedImage;

public class MapLayer extends TiledLayer {
    private int canvasWidth;
    private int canvasHeight;

    private static int[][] maps =  {
            { 1, 1, 1, 1, 1, 1, 1, 1, 1, 1 },
            { 1, 5, 1, 1, 5, 1, 1, 1, 5, 5 },
            { 1, 1, 1, 1, 1, 1, 1, 1, 1, 1 },
            { 1, 1, 1, 1, 1, 1, 1, 4, 1, 1 },
            { 1, 4, 1, 1, 1, 4, 1, 1, 1, 1 },
            { 1, 1, 1, 4, 1, 1, 1, 1, 1, 1 },
            { 1, 1, 1, 4, 1, 1, 1, 1, 1, 1 },
            { 1, 1, 1, 1, 1, 1, 1, 1, 1, 1 },
            { 1, 1, 1, 1, 4, 4, 1, 1, 4, 1 },
            { 1, 1, 1, 1, 1, 1, 1, 1, 1, 1 },
            { 1, 1, 1, 1, 1, 1, 1, 1, 1, 1 },
            { 1, 1, 1, 1, 3, 3, 3, 1, 1, 1 }
        };

    public MapLayer(String imagePath, int canvasWidth, int canvasHeight) {
        super(imagePath, maps, 32, 32, 10, 30);
        this.canvasWidth = canvasWidth;
        this.canvasHeight = canvasHeight;
    }

    public void draw(Graphics g) {
        for(int i=0;i<maps.length;i++)
        {
            for(int j=0;j<maps[i].length;j++)
            {
                int x=j*tiledWidth;
                int y=i*tiledHeight;
                g.setClip(x,y,tiledWidth,tiledHeight);
                g.drawImage(image, x-(maps[i][j]-1)*tiledWidth, y, null);
            }
        }
    }
}
```

Map2Layer.java in package com.state.cases;

```java
import java.awt.*;
import java.awt.image.BufferedImage;

public class Map2Layer extends TiledLayer {
    private int canvasWidth;
    private int canvasHeight;
    private static int[][] maps = {
        { 1, 1, 1, 1, 1, 1, 1, 1, 1, 1 },
        { 1, 5, 1, 1, 5, 1, 1, 1, 5, 5 },
        { 1, 1, 1, 1, 1, 1, 1, 1, 1, 1 },
        { 1, 1, 1, 1, 1, 1, 1, 4, 1, 1 },
        { 1, 4, 1, 1, 1, 4, 1, 5, 1, 1 },
        { 1, 1, 1, 4, 1, 1, 1, 1, 1, 1 },
        { 1, 1, 5, 4, 1, 1, 1, 1, 1, 1 },
        { 1, 1, 1, 1, 1, 1, 5, 1, 1, 1 },
        { 1, 1, 5, 1, 4, 4, 1, 1, 4, 1 },
        { 1, 1, 1, 1, 1, 1, 1, 1, 1, 1 },
        { 1, 1, 1, 5, 1, 1, 1, 1, 1, 1 },
        { 1, 1, 1, 1, 3, 3, 3, 1, 1, 1 },
        { 1, 1, 3, 1, 1, 1, 1, 5, 1, 1 }
    };

    public Map2Layer(String imagePath, int canvasWidth, int canvasHeight) {
        super(imagePath, maps, 32, 32, 10, 30);
        this.canvasWidth = canvasWidth;
        this.canvasHeight = canvasHeight;
    }

    public void draw(Graphics g) {
        for(int i=0;i<maps.length;i++)
        {
            for(int j=0;j<maps[i].length;j++)
            {
                int x=j*tiledWidth;
                int y=i*tiledHeight;
                g.setClip(x,y,tiledWidth,tiledHeight);
                g.drawImage(image, x-(maps[i][j]-1)*tiledWidth, y, null);
            }
        }
    }
}
```

MapContext.java in package com.state.cases;

```
import java.util.*;

public class MapContext {
   private LinkedList<TiledLayer> tiledLayerList=new LinkedList<TiledLayer>();
   private int index;

   public MapContext(){
   }

   public void addMap(TiledLayer tiledLayer){
      tiledLayerList.add(tiledLayer);
   }

   //Switch to the next map layer
   public TiledLayer next(){
      if(index >= tiledLayerList.size())
      {
         index =0;
      }
      TiledLayer tiledLayer = tiledLayerList.get(index);
      index++;
      return tiledLayer;
   }
}
```

```java
import java.awt.*;
import java.awt.image.BufferedImage;
import javax.swing.JPanel;

public class Canvas extends JPanel  implements Runnable{
    private boolean isRun = true;
    private boolean isInit = false;
    private int canvasWidth;
    private int canvasHeight;
    private TiledLayer mapLayer;
    private MapContext mapContext;
    private int time;

    public Canvas() {
        this.setLayout(null);
        this.setBackground(Color.WHITE);
    }

    private void  init(){
        mapContext = new MapContext();

            //Add all map layers to MapConext
        mapContext.addMap(new
MapLayer("images/map.png",this.canvasWidth,this.canvasHeight));
        mapContext.addMap(new
Map2Layer("images/map2.png",this.canvasWidth,this.canvasHeight));
        mapLayer = mapContext.next();
        new Thread(this).start();
    }

    protected void paintComponent(Graphics g) {
        this.canvasWidth = this.getWidth();
        this.canvasHeight = this.getHeight();
        if(!isInit){
            init();
            isInit = true;
        }
        super.paintComponent(g);
        drawMap(g);
    }
```

```java
public void drawMap(Graphics g){
    mapLayer.draw(g);
    time++;
    if(time == 20){ //Switch to the next map after redrawing 20 times
        mapLayer = mapContext.next();
    }
}

public void run() {
    while(isRun){
        try {
            Thread.sleep(100); //Sleep for 200 milliseconds to redraw the background
            Canvas.this.repaint();
        } catch (InterruptedException e) {
            e.printStackTrace();
        }
    }
}
}
```

3. Create a Test class : TestState.java in package com.state.game;

canvas.setFocusable(true): Set focus to activate keyboard events
canvas.requestFocus(): Set focus to activate keyboard events

```java
import java.awt.BorderLayout;
import javax.swing.JFrame;

public class TestState {

    public static void main(String[] args) {
        JFrame frame = new JFrame("Design Pattern State");
        Canvas canvas = new Canvas();
        frame.add(canvas, BorderLayout.CENTER);
        frame.setSize(300, 350);
        canvas.setFocusable(true);
        frame.setVisible(true);
        canvas.requestFocus();
    }
}
```

Right click TestState.java and then Run as -> Java Application Result:
Show first map layer: MapLayer

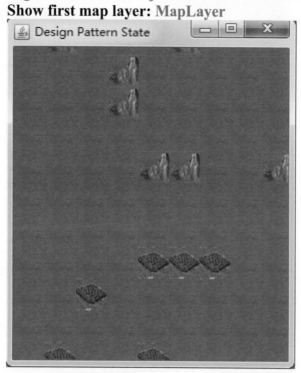

After redraw 20 times switch to show the second map layer: Map2Layer.

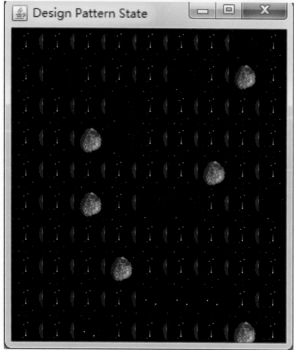

Proxy Pattern Principle

Static Proxy Pattern : An object representing another object. Provide a surrogate or placeholder for another object to control access to it.

1. Example: Clients buy a house and a car through an agency(ProxyCompany)

Analysis:
1. Create an interface: Buyer and then create 2 methods: buyHouse(),buyCar()
2. Create an implementation class: Client to buy house and buy car.
3. Create an implementation class: ProxyCompany to agent Client to buy house and buy car.

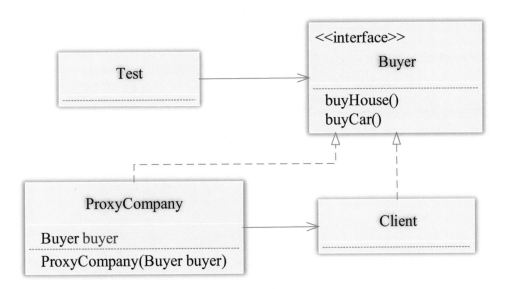

Buyer.java **in package com.proxy.principle;**

```
public interface Buyer {

    void buyHouse();
    void buyCar();
}
```

Client.java in package com.proxy.principle;

```java
public class Client implements Buyer {

    public void buyHouse() {
        System.out.println("I want to buy a house");
    }

    public void buyCar() {
        System.out.println("I want to buy a car");
    }
}
```

ProxyCompany.java in package com.proxy.principle;

```java
public class ProxyCompany implements Buyer {
    private Buyer buyer;

    public ProxyCompany(Buyer buyer) {
        this.buyer = buyer;
    }

    @Override
    public void buyHouse() {
        System.out.println("Prepare information and pay deposit");
        buyer.buyHouse();
        System.out.println("Decoration and settled");
    }

    @Override
    public void buyCar() {
        System.out.println("Determine the model of car and pay the deposit");
        buyer.buyCar();
        System.out.println("Pick up the car and go home");
    }
}
```

Test.java in package com.proxy.principle;

```java
public class Test {

    public static void main(String[] args) {
        Buyer buyer = new Client();

        ProxyCompany proxy= new ProxyCompany(buyer);
        proxy.buyHouse();

        System.out.println("--------------------------");

        proxy.buyCar();
    }
}
```

Right click Test.java and then Run as -> Java Application Result:

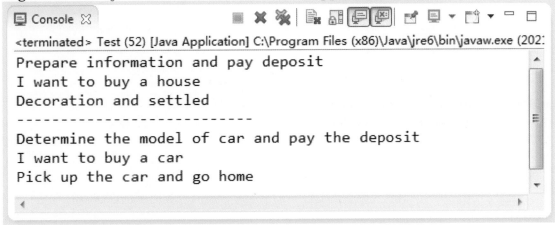

Disadvantages of Static Proxy Pattern: Once the interface changes, the proxy class must be modified.
We use the dynamic proxy provided by JDK to solve this problem

Dynamic Proxy: In dynamic proxy, we no longer need to manually create proxy classes, we only need to write a dynamic processor DynamicProxyHandler implements InvocationHandler. The real proxy object is dynamically created for us by the JDK at runtime.

The easiest way to do this is to use the java.lang.reflect.Proxy class, which is part of the JDK. That class can create a proxy class or directly an instance of it. The use of the Java built-in proxy is easy. All you need to do is implement a java.lang.InvocationHandler, so that the proxy object can invoke it. The InvocationHandler interface is extremely simple. It contains only one method: invoke(). When invoke() is invoked, the arguments contain the original object, which is proxied, the method that was invoked (as a reflection Method object) and the object array of the original arguments. A sample code demonstrates the use:

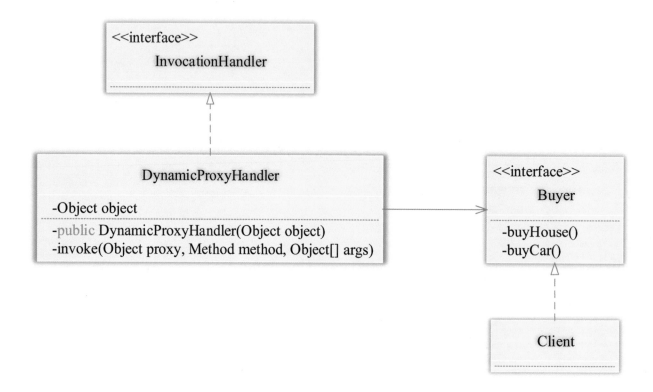

DynamicProxyHandler.java in package com.proxy.principle;

```java
import java.lang.reflect.*;
public class DynamicProxyHandler implements InvocationHandler {
  private Object object;

  public DynamicProxyHandler(final Object object) {
    this.object = object;
  }

  public Object invoke(Object proxy, Method method, Object[] args) throws Throwable {
    System.out.println("Prepare information and pay deposit");
    Object result = method.invoke(object, args);
    System.out.println("Pick up it and go home");
    return result;
  }
}
```

Create a test class: **TestDynamicProxy.java in package com.proxy.principle;**

```java
import java.lang.reflect.*;
public class TestDynamicProxy {
  public static void main(String[] args) {
      Buyer buyer = new Client();
      Buyer proxy = (Buyer) Proxy.newProxyInstance(Buyer.class.getClassLoader(), new
          Class[]{Buyer.class}, new DynamicProxyHandler(buyer));

      proxy.buyHouse();
      System.out.println("--------------------------");
      proxy.buyCar();
    }
}
```

Right click **TestDynamicProxy.java** **and then** **Run as -> Java Application** **Result:**

```
Console ⊠
Prepare information and pay deposit
I want to buy a house
Pick up it and go home
--------------------------
Prepare information and pay deposit
I want to buy a car
Pick up it and go home
```

Proxy Pattern Case

1. In AOP aspect-oriented programming, use dynamic proxy to read bean.xml file to instantiate objects

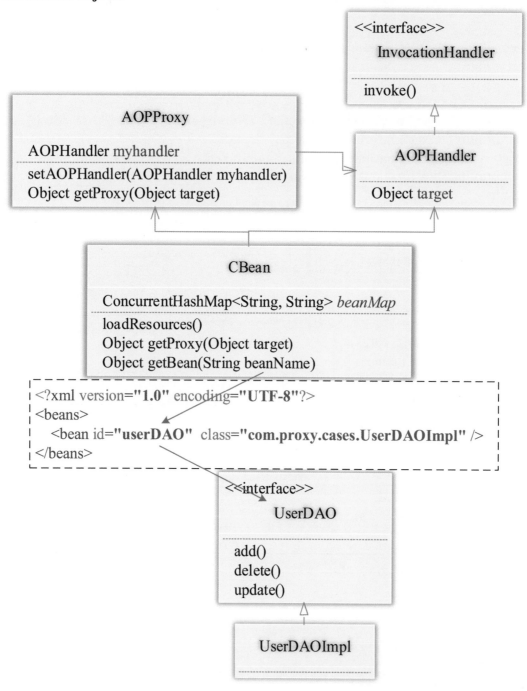

Create **bean.xml** in src

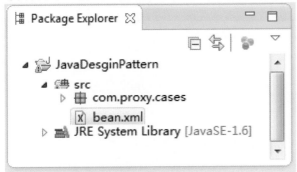

```xml
<?xml version="1.0" encoding="UTF-8"?>
<beans>
  <bean id="userDAO"  class="com.proxy.cases.UserDAOImpl" />
</beans>
```

Download the jar package for parsing XML

dom4j-1.6.1.jar
jaxen-1.1-beta-6.jar

http://en.verejava.com/download.jsp?id=1

add jar to Project

dom4j-1.6.1.jar , jaxen-1.1-beta-6.jar

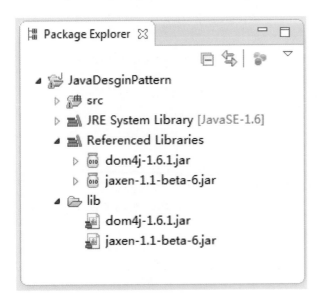

Create all classes in project test/com.proxy.cases

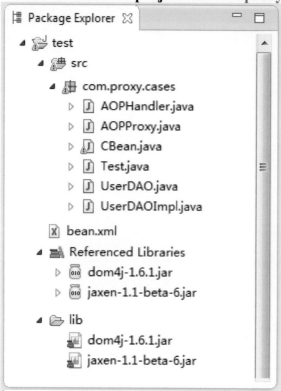

AOPHandler.java in package com.proxy.cases;

```java
import java.lang.reflect.*;

public class AOPHandler implements InvocationHandler {
    private Object target;

    public void setTarget(Object target) {
        this.target = target;
    }

    @Override
    public Object invoke(Object proxy, Method method, Object[] args) throws Throwable {
        System.out.println("before");
        Object returnObj = method.invoke(target, args);
        System.out.println("after");
        return returnObj;
    }
}
```

AOPProxy.java in package com.proxy.cases;

```java
import java.lang.reflect.Proxy;

public class AOPProxy {

    private AOPHandler myhandler;

    public void setAOPHandler(AOPHandler myhandler) {
        this.myhandler = myhandler;
    }

    public Object getProxy(Object target) {
        return Proxy.newProxyInstance(AOPProxy.class.getClassLoader(),
target.getClass().getInterfaces(), myhandler);
    }
}
```

UserDAO.java in package com.proxy.cases;

```java
public interface UserDAO {

    public boolean add();

    public boolean delete();

    public boolean update();
}
```

UserDAOImpl.java in package com.proxy.cases;

```java
public class UserDAOImpl implements UserDAO {

    public UserDAOImpl() {

    }

    @Override
    public boolean add() {
        System.out.println("Add User");
        return false;
    }

    @Override
    public boolean delete() {
        System.out.println("Delete User");
        return false;
    }

    @Override
    public boolean update() {
        System.out.println("Update User");
        return false;
    }
}
```

CBean.java in package com.proxy.cases;

```java
import java.io.*;
import java.util.List;
import java.util.concurrent.ConcurrentHashMap;
import org.dom4j.*;
public class CBean {
    private static ConcurrentHashMap<String, String> beanMap = new
ConcurrentHashMap<String, String>();

    static {
        loadResources();
    }

    public static void loadResources() {
        InputStream is = null;
        try {
            SAXReader reader = new SAXReader();
            Object obj = new Object();
            String classAbsolutePath = obj.getClass().getResource("/").getPath() + "/bean.xml";
            String filePath = classAbsolutePath;
            is = new FileInputStream(filePath);

            if (is == null) {
                return;
            }
            Document doc = reader.read(is);
            List<Element> elementList = doc.selectNodes("/beans/bean");
            for (Element element : elementList) {
                String id = element.attributeValue("id");
                String clazz = element.attributeValue("class");
                beanMap.put(id, clazz);
            }
        } catch (Exception e) {
            e.printStackTrace();
        } finally {
            try {
                is.close();
            } catch (IOException e) {
                e.printStackTrace();
            }
        }
    }
}
```

```java
private static Object getProxy(Object target) {
    AOPHandler myhandler = new AOPHandler();
    myhandler.setTarget(target);
    AOPProxy proxy = new AOPProxy();
    proxy.setAOPHandler(myhandler);
    return proxy.getProxy(target);
}

public static Object getBean(String beanName) {
    String clazzName = beanMap.get(beanName);
    Class clazz = null;
    Object obj = null;
    try {
        clazz = Class.forName(clazzName);
        obj = clazz.newInstance();
    } catch (ClassNotFoundException e) {
        e.printStackTrace();
    } catch (InstantiationException e) {
        e.printStackTrace();
    } catch (IllegalAccessException e) {
        e.printStackTrace();
    }
    return getProxy(obj);
}
}
```

Create a test class: Test.java **in package** com.proxy.cases;

```java
public class Test {

    public static void main(String[] args) {
        UserDAO userDao = (UserDAO)CBean.getBean("userDAO");

        userDao.add();
        System.out.println("--------------------------");

        userDao.delete();
        System.out.println("--------------------------");

        userDao.update();
    }
}
```

Right click Test.java **and then** Run as -> Java Application **Result:**

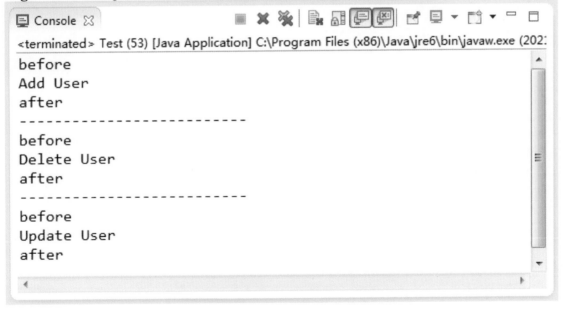

Interpreter Pattern Principle

Interpreter pattern: is the behavior pattern of the class. Given a language, the interpreter pattern can define a representation of its grammar and provide an interpreter at the same time. The client can use this interpreter to interpret the sentence.

1. Example: Use interpreter pattern to implement addition and subtraction operations

Analysis:
1. Create an abstract class: Expression and then create a method: interpret() to interpret addition and subtraction operations
2. Create an implementation class: Constant as the operand.
3. Create an implementation class: Add to implement addition operation.

```
public Add(Expression exp1, Expression exp2) {
    this.exp1 = exp1;
    this.exp2 = exp2;
}

public int interpret() {

    return exp1.interpret() + exp2.interpret();
}
```

4. Create an implementation class: Sub to implement subtraction operation.

```
public Sub(Expression exp1, Expression exp2) {
    this.exp1 = exp1;
    this.exp2 = exp2;
}

public int interpret() {
    return exp1.interpret() - exp2.interpret();
}
```

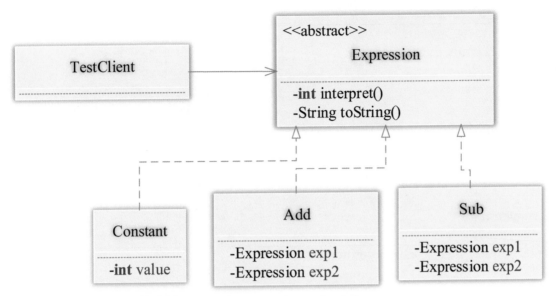

Expression.java in package com. interpreter.principle;

```
public abstract  class Expression {

   public abstract int interpret();

   public abstract String toString();
}
```

Constant.java in package com. interpreter.principle;

```
public class Constant extends Expression {
   private int value;

   public Constant(int value){
      this.value = value;
   }

   public int interpret() {
      return value;
   }

   public String toString() {
      return new Integer(value).toString();
   }
}
```

Add.java in package com. interpreter.principle;

```java
public class Add extends Expression {
    protected Expression exp1;
    protected Expression exp2;

    public Add(Expression exp1, Expression exp2) {
        this.exp1 = exp1;
        this.exp2 = exp2;
    }

    public int interpret() {

        return exp1.interpret() + exp2.interpret();
    }

    @Override
    public String toString() {
        return "(" + exp1.toString() + " + " + exp2.toString() + ")";
    }
}
```

Sub.java in package com. interpreter.principle;

```java
public class Sub extends Expression {
    protected Expression exp1;
    protected Expression exp2;

    public Sub(Expression exp1, Expression exp2) {
        this.exp1 = exp1;
        this.exp2 = exp2;
    }

    public int interpret() {
        return exp1.interpret() - exp2.interpret();
    }

    public String toString() {
        return "(" + exp1.toString() + " - " + exp2.toString() + ")";
    }
}
```

TestClient.java in package com. interpreter.principle;

```java
public class TestClient {

    public static void main(String[] args) {
        Constant c1 = new Constant(5);
        Constant c2 = new Constant(3);
        Constant c3 = new Constant(6);
        Constant c4 = new Constant(2);
        Expression exp = new Add(new Add(c3, c2), new Sub(c4, c1));
        System.out.println(exp.toString() + " = " + exp.interpret());
    }
}
```

Right click TestClient.java and then Run as -> Java Application Result:

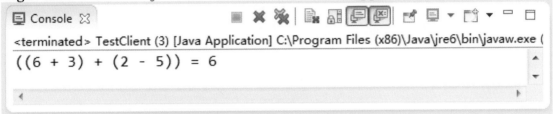

```
Console ⊠
<terminated> TestClient (3) [Java Application] C:\Program Files (x86)\Java\jre6\bin\javaw.exe (
((6 + 3) + (2 - 5)) = 6
```

Printed in Great Britain
by Amazon

83774692R00156